I CAME TO HELP YOU KNOW

A compilation of the extraordinary experiences of an ordinary woman

ROSEMARY M. LAWSON

ISBN: 978057586571_14-79

Library of Congress Subject Headings:

Meditation

Prophetic dreams

Psychic warnings

Synchronicity

Spirituality for skeptics

Ghosts

Skeptical mystic

New Wings Publishers

Wakefield, Massachusetts,

U. S. A.

Acknowledgements

First, thanks to Betty Allenbrook Wiberg, for your wonderful illustrations of my stories! And to the rest of the Wibergs, for your critiques and suggestions; thank you for those comments that made this book so much more easily understood.

Next, thanks go to Kevin Lawson, who provided critical technical assistance. I would have been stopped in my tracks so many times without your help! Thank you so much!

Then to Maria Almeida for my wonderful logo! It is so perfect for the spirit of New Wings Publishers!

Then to Maureen O'Brien Ruivo; thanks for going through the long slog of the final layout and grammar checks with me, as well as all the endless details about ISBN numbers, and final book formats! What a process!

I am very grateful to Charlene Maguire for my beautiful cover, and to Jean Wallace, my photographer, for finding the gentle Rosey in her lens.

Finally, thanks so much to Suzanne Lahna and to Tricia Lawson for your perceptive editorial suggestions! I learned a lot from you.

In all the years since I first made the contents of my Journal available to a few of my friends and family, thanks to you who raised a question that helped me make a story less confusing. Or to you who told me that a particular story that helped you understand some mystical event in your own life. Your comments have helped me persevere to the point of publication!

I love you all so much! Here is the final version, thanks to your encouragement!

Contents

Foreword

I am a skeptical mystic... but that's an oxymoron. A mystic, according to Webster's New World Dictionary, is one who believes "that it is possible to achieve communion with God through contemplation and love without the medium of human reason." Also "One who professes to undergo mystical experiences by which [she or] he comprehends truths beyond human understanding." That would be my prayer —that I could have such experiences and that the experiences I have had do lead me to greater truths.

A skeptic, of course, is one who is "not easily persuaded or convinced; doubting; questioning." That would be me, too!

Oh, dear! Well, I have had experiences that are "beyond human understanding." The problem is that I often don't understand the mystical truths that are supposed to lurk therein. But the experiences are real. And when I meditate about the experience, I sometimes get an answer about what happened that feels both deeply satisfying and real.

And I know what I have experienced happened to me as an adult when I was sober and not under duress.

So, I meditate about the experiences. Sometimes that only evokes more experiences, but I add them to the list, and keep meditating. I know I belong in the meditative space.

And I read about the different aspects of meditation, spirituality, theology, life after life, psychic phenomena, and the alpha brain state. I read books by new age physicists, until they get so far out on their limbs that I scurry back to the relative safety of a good book by a psychic spiritual healer. (See "Ex Libris," later in this book, for my favorites.)

And I share my experiences with trusted therapists of various stripes who I have worked with over the years: talk therapists of the Jungian persuasion, of the Rogerian school, one whose specialty was Neuro-Linguistic Programming. My Reiki body workers, my music therapist, and my other teachers. One minister and two meditation mentors.

To understand these stories, it will help you to know these baseline facts about my life: I was married for 14 years during which time I had two sons, Rick and Kevin. After I was divorced, I met my soul mate, Tom. And after Tom died of cancer at a very young age, I eventually ended up with a third major partner. You only meet him briefly in these stories when I realize that I have to leave the house we had bought together and shared for 10 years, so you don't need to know his name. He was not a soul mate.

I am really a very ordinary person, not a natural-born psychic, but I have had these mystical experiences anyway. If similar things happen to you, be peaceful with yourself. If others don't believe you (hmmm...understatement, right?) don't pester them too much with your beliefs. But don't deny your experiences, just because others do not believe. Keep trying to find somebody who will validate what happened to you by sharing their mystical experiences. Join a Swedenborg Reading Group, a meditation group, or an Edgar Cayce "Search for God" group. Good luck and God bless!

Rosemary M. Lawson

New Wings Publishers

Wakefield, Massachusetts   November 2019

1 Strange Happenings

I had some unusual things happen in my early years, but I am not prepared for how often they appear after I am divorced. I also start meditating during this period. Is this a coincidence? Could those events be connected?

The Stop Light that Screamed

It is early evening. I have just finished a lovely, leisurely dinner with a close friend at a nice restaurant that is a couple miles from home. It is on a road I am very familiar with, I don't drink, so what happens next has nothing to do with liquor, and it is still early. In fact, it is that gorgeous long light of a New England summer's evening.

In Massachusetts some traffic lights have a specific phase that allows traffic to turn left; the light looks like a green arrow pointing left. At those intersections, it is illegal to turn left without that green arrow.

You know how you become familiar with the pattern of stop lights on roads that you frequent? You are aware that traffic in your lane will get a delayed green, and only a certain number of cars will be able to get through the green arrow for a left turn. You get so you know how long the light pauses in its amber phase, before it turns to red, and so on.

I am going to turn onto the highway, but I need that left arrow in order to do so. The light turns in my favor just as I approach it, but then, so suddenly that it scares me, the light turns to red with a screaming WHAM!!

I screech to a stop, startled, and try to figure it out: Was there a real "wham" that I could hear with my ears? How could that be true? But there was a psychic jolt from that light that made me jam on my brakes, as though there was something immediately in front of me that I had to avoid hitting with my car.

Now, this is Massachusetts, well known for traffic that makes left-hand turns on the amber light, and I have been known to follow that particular traffic flow myself from time to time, but not this time. That stoplight was screaming at me to stop!

It does not speak to the slinky red sports car in the lane to my right, however; that car goes screeching around me and up onto the access ramp to the highway. I notice the car, but shrug at the driver's action. He is just being a normal Massachusetts driver.

So, I sit through the light, wondering why it went red so fast (far under its usual amount of time at the amber stage), and why I perceived it to be such a startlingly RED light.

Then I get my green arrow and drive onto the highway. Within a couple of miles, I am up to full speed, and traveling in the far-left lane. As I go over the crown of the next hill, I am startled by something obscure up ahead in the roadway that I can't make sense of.

I see what looks like a cloud of smoke or dust in the roadway. I slack off my speed, and then start pumping my brakes as a warning to the cars behind me. The traffic ahead is stopped all across the four-lane highway. I see nothing but bright red brake lights!

By the time I approach the other cars, most are stopped, but there is a clear path in the far-left lane. As the two cars ahead of me ease through it, I follow them. There is a lot of trash in the roadway... small pieces of stuff that don't make any particular sense, but which I don't want to run over for fear they will cut my tires.

But what I see as I get abreast of the stopped cars is horrifying. There is that same slinky red sports car that had squealed around me at that red stoplight. Suddenly, I figure out what had happened: that car had lost control at this point on the roadway and swerved up onto the Jersey barriers that are immediately off the road on the left. It shed parts of itself along the way then swung back into the roadway, hitting two other cars. It finally stopped on its roof. The driver of the sports car had been thrown from his car and is lying on his back in the roadway, lit up by all the stopped cars around him. And lying much too still.

I pull over to the far side of the road and sit in my car, near tears and trembling. Had I gone through that stoplight, the one that screamed at me and turned red too fast, I would have been the car immediately behind the red car, and would have been in the middle of that accident.

After the police and emergency vehicles go their way, I start toward home again. Thank you for stopping me at that light, Angels. It must be that I still have work to do on this planet.

Unheeded Warnings?

The biggest problems with psychic messages are translating them and knowing which ones to believe. My marriage lasted for fourteen years before it dissolved in infidelity, but I had what certainly could be seen as two warnings before I was married.

My then boyfriend and I were so smitten that we got married after we had known each other only seven months. Of course, this means that we started planning the wedding after we had been together only two or three months! The two psychic events I had at the time were vivid enough so I still remember them, many years later. But I have trouble labeling them as clear warnings. On the other hand, when I said that to a close friend, she burst out laughing.

My boyfriend has an aunt who loves to shop, and she declared that she knows everybody in the jewelry business in downtown Boston. Therefore, it is her duty to take the two of us to buy our wedding rings. She has a lot of jewelry, so I can't refute that aspect of her taking on this task, but she is pretty bossy, and I am not thrilled about the arrangement. Her bossiness wins out, and the three of us traipse downtown on a lovely Spring afternoon.

She impresses me with her knowledge of where to go: she takes us to a place that does not even have a store front on the main street at all. It is inside what looks like a regular office building, along with a lot of other jewelry stores. However, once we get inside the shop, it looks just like any other jewelry store I've ever been in, so we go over to the counter where they display all their rings.

Auntie tries again to pressure us into buying a diamond, but our budget doesn't have room for one, and she isn't offering to give it to us as a wedding present. So, we move on to the two wedding bands.

Once again, she goes right for the most expensive pair displayed, but my sweetheart and I just want the plain gold bands. It is at this moment that I faint, right in the store. I just slide to the floor in a heap.

That action gets a lot of attention from everyone in the immediate vicinity! And it causes me a huge amount of embarrassment! A chair is found for me to sit on, someone brings a glass of water, and people keep wanting to call an ambulance…there is chaos everywhere!

The water helps, and I keep trying to normalize the event as people around me ply me with questions: Maybe I haven't eaten enough that day? Is it too hot? Have I been exposed to a flu? No, no, I say, I am fine….

Eventually we pick out our plain gold bands, and leave.

The next warning, if it is one, comes the morning of my wedding: I cannot stop crying. I am not sobbing, but I have tears sliding down my cheeks all morning long.

Mom alternates between concern about whether I am alright and frustration that nothing seems to stop the tears. The photographer manages to find poses for his bride by draping the veil over my face, and turning my face so I am not in bright light. But the tears are unstoppable!

Eventually we all leave for the church hoping I can get my act together sooner rather than later! When I walk down the aisle, my face is still wet with tears, but by the time the ceremony is over, I feel a huge sense of relief, and I am fine! The photograph of the two of us walking down the aisle looks like we are flying!

So, were they psychic warnings that were in effect for fourteen years before the divorce they may have predicted actually materialized?

The Rocking Chair that Rocks

The rocking chair is mine, the generous gift of my mother-in-law the first Christmas I am in the family.

"It's for rocking the baby," she says. "Every baby needs to be rocked, and you don't have a rocker."

It is beautiful! Glistening black, with gold-toned pears and peaches, grapes, and leaves stenciled on the head-rest, and fine gold lines highlighting the turnings on the legs.

And it has a good sway —long rockers, gently curved, give easy sweep back and forth, back and forth, as I do, indeed, rock my first baby.

Through nursing, and comfort-times, and storybooks. Through tears, and fevers, and teething.

It becomes my chair, by unspoken family consensus, the way those things happen. And with my second babe coming, long summer-hot months I've rocked my growing body and the restless babe inside to comfort each so both could catch a little rest. Those last heavy weeks, I've sat by the open window, rocking to make a breeze when there is none, my little cocker spaniel at my feet.

It is the '60s. Babies are born in the hospital, with fathers firmly excluded, and even the mother anesthetized against the event. Because of an unfriendly gene shared by the women in my family, I experience delayed births and I have been in non-productive labor for nine days. Eventually the doctor decides I need some help.

So, on a hot Sunday afternoon, I am in the hospital, and the expectant father and grandmother sit chatting in the living room at home, waiting for the doctor's call. It is that stillness of late August: the curtains at the windows cannot detect a breeze.

My little cocker spaniel has been curled, asleep, in her usual spot at the foot of my rocker. She gets up, and whining lightly, paces small circles in the rug, tail-wagging all the way.

Then, though she has never been trained to hunt, she goes into point: paw raised, stub-tail out straight, and nose pointing at the empty rocking chair.

Her actions attract the attention of the two adults, and they watch idly, then stare as the empty chair silently begins to rock by itself. Back and forth, back and forth, in nice, slow, easy sweeps.

It lasts no more than a few minutes. Then the dog gives a contented sigh and settles back to sleep in her spot at the chair's foot. Expectant father and grandmother are rooted in their seats; they haven't spoken during the whole event, or hardly even breathed.

Suddenly the spell of the chair, and the silence, are broken by the ring of the telephone. It is the doctor: "Congratulations, Father! You have another son."

Once I bring my tiny son home, Grandma tells me the story of the rocking chair. And I add it to my collection of wonder-filled events.

Trouble on the Trip to Vermont

It is a Friday night in the summertime of 1974, and everybody, including me, is trying to get out of town. I am heading north, up to Lake Champlain where we will be celebrating my son's twelfth birthday.

I am eager to see my boys, as it has been a long month of separation, with me in Boston desperately trying to find a job as a teacher while a July headline in The Boston Globe informs me: "7000 Unemployed teachers in the Commonwealth." The content of the article states that the number does not include teachers who are employed in insurance companies, or working retail or wait-staff jobs in restaurants. That is not why I just got my Master's degree in education! This employment situation is daunting.

So, in Friday traffic, my big 100,000-miles-plus station wagon is hurtling northward along with a few thousand of my best friends (that would be the other Massachusetts drivers, known world-wide for their lack of courtesy).

We hit a huge thunderstorm just at the point where the highway drops down to two lanes, with hardly any shoulder. And the storm is horrific: heavy, wind-driven rain that the wipers can barely move around enough to allow me a momentary glimpse of what is ahead. There are many strikes of brilliant lightening that frighten and momentarily blind all of us, followed immediately by roars of thunder you can feel in your chest. The radio promises that we are driving right into the storm, and won't get out the other side for over an hour, possibly more.

It is raining so hard that I close the vent window, which I usually leave open to provide a place to flick my cigarette. But rain is pouring in through even the smallest crack. So, I shut the car up tight, and drive.

I have the radio on, and am moving slightly to the music, when I suddenly realize I am staring at the windshield wipers instead of looking through the window to the road ahead.

"Stop that!" I tell myself, curtly! "Watch the car ahead of you!"

That chide only works for a moment. I find myself doing it again. And again, I scold myself: "Cut it out! Watch the traffic!!"

When I check my rear-view window, I realize that all the windows of the car are steamed up. Then I am immediately back staring at the wipers! "Cut it out! You can get killed this way!"

What is wrong with me? I can't seem to concentrate on my driving! With a feeling of horror, I realize I have highway hypnosis! I am being hypnotized by the wipers, and I can't seem to get away from the effect they are having on me.

I think of pulling over, but there is only a small half car-width shoulder, and with the poor visibility I realize that some other car would follow me right off the road. I throw the air conditioner on high and aim one vent directly at my face. Then I decide it is better to get wet than not have some fresh air coming into the car, so I open the window a crack.

The fresh air helps, but second by second I keep slipping back into staring at the windshield, so I turn the radio on high, and start singing at the top of my lungs to whatever inane rock song comes on. Anything to stay alert.

Just then, I see a highway road sign for a rest area, two miles ahead. "Oh, thank God!" I think. "I can make it two miles…" but it is the longest two miles I have ever driven.

I pull into the rest area, lock all four doors of the car, turn off the motor, and simply drop down across the front bench seat. I immediately collapse into a deep sleep.

I wake up groggy, aching from having slept on my side for so long… how long was that? I am shocked to realize I have slept for four hours! Oh, dear! The folks at home will be worried about me. Delightfully, the storm has worked itself out and it is a beautiful cool evening. I call home from the rest area, tell them that the storm delayed traffic, but I am on my way.

A cup of coffee from the rest stop canteen helps. And I have all the windows open for the rest of the trip, enjoying the beautiful summer evening.

For reasons I don't understand, every time I sit down all weekend, I fall asleep. I sleep on the dock, down on the beach, I sleep on the screened porch, I sleep in the big chairs by the fireplace … I'm having a great time with my family, and I don't want to nap, but I simply can't stay awake.

Sunday comes too soon; I need to drive that five hours back to Boston. Reluctantly, I get under way in the early afternoon. Most of the trip is freeway, but there is one toll section of the highway. As I pull into the toll booth, a very pleasant toll taker says: "Do you know that you're pouring exhaust out of the middle of the car? You better get that checked —you could die of carbon monoxide poisoning!"

I look at him with my mouth agape. So that is it! With all the windows shut on Friday, that carbon monoxide was filling the car, and trying very hard to kill me on my stormy drive northward.

The next morning, I bring the car in, and my mechanic confirms: "I could put my fist through the hole in your muffler! You've got to get this fixed right away!"

I am shocked. I thought that if you have even a tiny hole in your muffler you know about it, because you sound like a tank in low gear. Apparently not always!

Thank you, Angels, for prodding me so insistently on that very long, and very treacherous drive on Friday. I never gave anyone a better birthday present than struggling to stay awake on that trip! That also explains all those unplanned naps all weekend! It was the after effects of all that carbon monoxide!

By the time he got to be an adult, I told my son about that trip, so he would know that you can have a silent muffler problem. And also, so he would know how much I love him.

This event is one of the things I have meditated on repeatedly in the thirty some years since it happened. At that time, I was newly divorced and feeling a huge amount of shame. I was not only suicidal; I had decided that I would kill myself by driving that very same station wagon into a bridge abutment… I kept telling myself I would do it some day, but I couldn't most days because I had to do something for my boys.

I realize that the very instrument I had selected to end my life, caused me to fight for my life with every ounce of strength I could muster. I have to wonder where that strength came from. And as soon as I ask myself that question, I know the answer. I may call it "my Angels" to keep the tone light, or I may admit that it came from the Source of all help. I am humble and grateful.

And I try to figure out what other tasks I am supposed to be doing on the planet, since I am still having this glorious ride around the sun, year after year.

If Walls Could Talk

Almost two years previously I was divorced, and within ten days I lost my job as a public school teacher in New Jersey. It is the '70s, when schools are closing because of decreasing populations. I have decided to move up to Massachusetts, where my sisters live, in order to find a job there. That would also give me some emotional support as I try to put a new life together for myself and my two sons.

Eventually I find a teaching job in Massachusetts, and an apartment to move into. As that first year progresses, the house in New Jersey that had held the remains of my marriage finally sells, and I have enough down payment for a modest home.

I eventually find a house that beckons to me. Getting the bank loan is not easy, but they cave in when I protest that they are being sexist and threaten to get a lawyer from NOW. I triumphantly close on the house and we move all our belongings in.

It is with a sense of elation that I unpack box after box. By the end of the first day that we are in the new house, curtains and pictures are hung, and the kitchen, bathroom, and bedrooms are all unpacked! We have made great progress.

Eventually it is time for the boys to go off to their new bedrooms, and I am alone, still unpacking boxes of books, happy in my new space, but somehow restless. Apropos of nothing in particular, I stop my work and decide to go on a house tour.

I start in my bedroom. There is a pair of bi-fold louvered doors that close my bedroom off from the downstairs living room. I walk over to the doors and slide them shut.

I suddenly see a huge gouge in the soft pine and, at the same instance, see a man's hand holding a broken whiskey bottle and making the slashing gesture that had damaged the door.

I back off, stunned, shaking my head to clear it and trying to make sense of what I saw. The doors are stained dark brown, but the pale pine wood shows through very clearly where it was gouged by that broken bottle. A jagged white scar against the dark stain.

Still shaken by the violence and strength of that hand, and puzzled by the process that had allowed me to see it, I decide to tour the house thoroughly, and look for... I don't know what! I know that the couple who sold the house were divorcing. Now I also know that alcohol and violence were involved. Literally? A broken bottle? I shudder at the thought and hope it was a metaphor created by my mind.

I check the whole rest of the downstairs, without finding anything else troublesome. But once I get upstairs to the main living level, I find multiple other signs of the same kind of violent anger. Way down at the bottom of another door, there is a large, ugly place that is dented inward. Suddenly, I see the man's foot in the hiking boot that kicked it, smashing the plywood facade. In a hiking boot. I recognize it, but such vivid detail is startling. I don't own any hiking boots, or even know anybody who does. That is not a detail my own mind would have created.

By now the boys are fast asleep, so I take a flashlight and check their bedrooms, determined to see every inch of this strange house that is showing me so much more than I had looked for. Sure enough, another door is smashed in. And I suddenly "know" that that door had been swapped with the door across the hall.

At first, I can't make any sense of why the owners would have swapped the doors. I open and shut them both several times, trying to figure out why. Then I realize that swapping the doors puts the damaged side against the wall when the door is open. It was a ruse to avoid repairing the damage or buy a new door before selling the house! They hoped it would not be noticed during house inspections and they would not have to pay to fix it.

In another room, there is a broken pane of glass in a large window. A man's hand had slammed the window down so hard it cracked the glass. Again, that man's hand! I shudder and shake my head, trying to clear it. So much anger!

As I make my way throughout the house, I quietly ask that all traces of violence leave the property, and that we be allowed to live there peacefully. I don't realize it at the time, but I am following an ancient practice of blessing a home and invoking peace for its new inhabitants.

A lot happened in that house while we lived there, but not the violence that it had seen with its previous owners. If walls could talk, indeed!

That Old Bad Temper

My dreams are scolding me for my bad temper and quickness to flare in anger. Last night I had a complex dream about being in a big old Victorian-style house. There is a central stairwell with a grand staircase that spirals up and around, all the way to the third floor.

There is a woman standing on the first floor who is very angry and keeps getting angrier. As that happens, she grows taller by the minute…eventually getting as tall as the stairs on the third floor. She is yelling and scolding, and her voice resonates in the huge stairwell as if it were an echo chamber. The sound is deep inside my terrified body. I keep running up the stairs to get away from all that anger, but it doesn't matter. I can't get away from it or from her. I run from room to room on the third floor looking for someplace to hide: behind doors, inside closets, under beds, but nowhere is safe!

I wake in a cold sweat, frightened that the anger is going to get me. I suddenly realize that it is my anger, and it has gotten me. I'm certain my beloved therapist is going to agree with that conclusion.

My anger is at the combination of the divorce and losing my job! But my dreams do not approve of angry behavior. The anger in this dream has a self-righteousness to it, but that doesn't count for anything. I wake certain that anger is a form of violence and violence is never acceptable. Well, that fits with the reading I have been doing on spirituality! Oh dear! I have so very much to learn!

In Which Tom Meets Rosey

I met Tom at TNS —The Next Step —the singles club we both belong to. It is a Friday night party, and I have danced for hours. I am in a great mood and there is plenty of wonderful music on the phonograph. One woman who is watching the group of dancers comments: "How do you do it? Your feet haven't touched the floor for hours, and you don't even look winded!"

I smile and nod as I walk past her in the crowded kitchen. I am headed for the sink, and a tall glass of water. I may not be winded but I'm plenty thirsty!

As I push through the mob in the kitchen, I become aware that there is a pair of eyes that is following me, and drilling a hole in the back of my head. It isn't scary at all… just something to notice and wonder about. Who is watching my every move?

After I fill my glass, I start drinking, and slowly turn around, checking all the faces I can see, looking for those eyes that are still riveted on me. Ah-ha! There they are. He is a little taller than most of the folks in the room, and still intently studying my every move.

I decide to wander over to him, to see if I am as interested in him as he is in me! So, I make my way back through the mob, keeping my eyes looking back at his, matching stare for unblinking stare. When I get up to him, I smile and say "Hi! You've been watching me!"

Later he confesses that I totally threw him off guard by being so open. But that doesn't show at the moment. He says "Hi" back, and asks if I want to dance with him. You bet I do. He has a wonderful smile, his eyes twinkle, and I like his energy a lot.

As soon as I move into his arms, I feel safe and comfortable, as if I've known him for ages (lifetimes?) and as if I belong right there —inside his aura! We dance easily together. He is quite a bit taller than I, but everything about him feels easy, familiar, and right. When he asks if I would like to go out with him for dinner the next night, I happily agree, and give him my phone number. Everybody in this group has been invited to join the club by a current member, and everybody has been screened before they are admitted. So, there is no worry that he is secretly married, or that he is some kind of weirdo.

Don't get me wrong: there is a handful of delightfully weird people: artists, professional dancers, engineers who are so deep into their specialty that it takes the better part of an evening to figure out what they do… but they are likely to be that kind of wonderful, deeply committed "weird," not the dangerous weird.

I go home thrilled about the prospect of my date with Tom and exhausted from my long week at work, as well as my long night of dancing. I sleep soundly, but wake up the next morning with the emotions from a horrible dream. Emotionally I am a wreck, but I can't remember what about the dream got me so upset! I am just filled with a sense of dread.

I decide to call my older sister, who is President of the TNS group, to see if she had met Tom. I tell her about having met him, and about our planned date. And also, about the frightening dream that I can't remember. She suggests that when he calls to get directions to my place, I tell him about the dream, and say I am having second thoughts about meeting with him. She assures me that he will understand, and we will be able to talk it through.

So, when Tom does call, I tell him about my anxious feelings, and ask if we could break the date. I can hear that I have startled him; he takes a sharp breath, and then doesn't say anything for a couple of long minutes.

Finally, he asks very tentatively if we could still keep the date, but talk about my feelings in person, rather than try to figure them out on the phone. No pressure, he assures me... just time to work it out in person? I love the sound of his voice, and I am reminded of the way I felt when I met him: this man is gentle, caring, and safe. My anxious feelings evaporate, and I happily agree.

So, it's settled. He will pick me up and we will go to a local restaurant, where they have a live band on Saturday nights.

That night at the restaurant he is every bit a gentleman. We talk easily, swapping stories of how we had gotten to our current status in life, and ended up at TNS the night before. He has a wonderful sense of humor, but he's also gentle, and a good listener. What is not to like? I relax, and start having a wonderful time! We have finished our supper, and I suggest that we dance. I can't wait to get back in his arms.

As we step onto the dance floor and he holds me gently, I have the intense feeling of being wrapped up in his aura, just as I had the night before.

He feels totally safe, I feel totally at home, and when they play a slow dance after a few fast ones, I feel like I am falling in love, so totally and so happily that I just turn my face up to smile at him... and am rewarded with a gentle kiss. I have never fallen in love at first sight before, but I do this night. Completely and hopelessly in love.

Years later I answer my therapist's question about how we had met with this story. At the end, she asks if the disturbing dream the night before our first date could have foretold Tom's death. The question totally stops me in my tracks. Of course! That would have been a horrible dream! So bad that I couldn't admit to myself the next morning what the contents of the dream had actually been... and certainly totally outside the boundaries of any bad news dream I could imagine while awake.

My angels had tried to protect me, but they couldn't stop me from dancing happily into that relationship, with all the love that it would contain. And, actually, I would not have given up the joy and depth of the experiences that we shared. The hands-on healing, the hours and hours of shared meditation, working together creatively... it was all very precious. And then devastatingly sad watching Tom give in to the cancer that killed him. But he helped me grow in so many ways.

Of course, there were some tough times in that relationship, as well. Times when we couldn't agree how to handle an insurmountable problem that we faced. Times when the finances were so tight, we couldn't see our way through that month's bills. Times when my need to take care of my children conflicted with his need to be more carefree. But the Universe seemed to come through with a beautiful solution, time after glorious time!

They say that the depth of your loss cannot be more than the breadth of your love. We both grew enormously in that dimension. I am so very grateful for my soul mate's love.

Cue the Gulls

Tom is a photographer and has a fabulous eye. We are in Newport, Rhode Island, to photograph Tall Ships '76. The town is brim full of colorful people, the harbor is brim full of beautiful ships, and Tom is in his mettle. Two or three cameras (each with a different type of film) hang from his neck at all times, and I eventually get used to his grabbing one of them, and stopping just long enough to frame and shoot some wonderful sight. One such shot becomes part of our family folklore.

We are walking along a rough driveway between dilapidated 100-year old buildings close to the waterfront. There is a small grassy area right in front of us, in which are parked several shiny new motorcycles. Huge mechanical beasts that are somehow noisy even at rest. Right behind them is the whole harbor, full of spiky tall ships' masts.

Tom loves the contrast between the superfluous power implied by the bikes and the elegant structures of the masts with their furled sails that appear to be lined up behind the bikes. He pulls out a camera and sets the focus. Then, checking the sky, he says, "Cue the gulls!"

I roar with laughter. No sooner said, than a pair of them appear on the right, heading directly over the spot where Tom is shooting. "Here they come!" I say.

"Got 'em!" is the reply, as the camera clicks and with a huge grin, he throws his arm around me and we saunter on our way.

Dreams and Other Mysteries

What a gift dreams are! Funny, informative…

For a number of years after the divorce, I not only meditate regularly, I keep a dream journal. My Alpha life is rich with meaning, which it reveals only as long as I am diligent in honoring my dreams by writing them down in the middle of the night.

At this point, my father has one of his many heart attacks. I make some kind of emergency arrangements for my sons to stay home so they can go to school, and I leave Massachusetts for the hospital in upstate New York so I can be with my father. My sisters are also at the little hospital in the Catskills, but we don't know for how long. This uncertainty is always one of the agonizing aspects of a medical emergency. It is made many times worse when you have to travel to the hospital from a great distance.

Daddy is pretty sick and, of course, the doctors don't know what is going to happen. I am feeling really torn between returning home to my sons or staying in the motel near the hospital, in case Daddy goes into crisis and I am needed here. As day and night drag into another day and night, I decide to ask my dreams what I should do. The next morning, I distinctly remember having a dream, but I did not wake enough in the night to write it down. As soon as I stir the next morning, the dream becomes fuzzy, and I can't make sense of it. I don't dare leave.

So that evening I get very firm with my Alpha brain, and announce to myself as I go to sleep that "I want a dream to tell me what I should do, I want it to be clear, and I want to remember it!"

I don't get one dream. I get two.

First Dream

I am playing my grand piano and Maryot, my huge German Shepard, comes over to me and starts pawing at my hands. In my dream I yell at the top of my lungs: "Leave!" I shout. "Stop it! Go!"

I smile at the obvious clarity as I jot down my notes in my dream journal some time in the middle of the night. Then I roll over for some more sleep.

Second Dream

My two sisters and I are back being young children, and we are playing in the yard. It is fall, and somebody has done a lot of raking so there are piles of yellow, red, and orange leaves all around us. We suddenly start dancing in the piles, throwing armfuls of leaves up in the air, and singing and calling out: "And when we do leaves, we do leaves!"

The family laughs with me the next morning as I tell them the messages of my dreams. And I leave later in the day, confident that it is time for me to go home.

Postscript

Daddy did, indeed, recover so my presence at the hospital after that day was not needed. One more time, my dreams did more than give me accurate advice, they provided a silly pun in the process, as if to shrug and say, "Oh, come on! Ask for something a little harder, will you?"

Maryot and Our Spook

We all know we have a ghost in the house. He is very noisy, although not otherwise destructive. However, it is plenty unnerving to be sitting somewhere, speaking to the person you know you just heard come upstairs, only to get no reply… again! Because it was the disembodied energy that had just come noisily clomping up the stairs, not the family member you expected.

My sons, Rick and Kevin, are teenagers, and Tom is my partner at this point in our lives. His enormous German Shepard, Maryot, makes up the rest of the family; at least the rest of the family that we can all see.

Before we had Maryot, it was really unsettling for any one of us to believe we were alone in the house, only to hear clear footsteps walking down the hall, or up the stairs. More than one of us has picked up a baseball bat to fend off the housebreaker we thought we heard, only to find nobody there. Once we realize that we are only staring at an empty hallway or empty staircase where we had just heard the foot traffic, we usually relax about it.

Much better to come face to non-face with a spook than to come face to face with somebody who had broken into the house!

The house has two living rooms: one on the upstairs street level, and the other on the finished basement level, right next to the bedroom that Tom and I share. The lower living room also serves as Tom's audio/video production room, our project room, and a place for the adults to get away from the teenagers.

On one particular night, the downstairs living room is serving as Meeting Central. We are deep in a full-family meeting, trying to figure out schedules for the upcoming weeks.

Rick and I are facing the steps leading to the upstairs living area, while Kevin and Tom have their backs to the steps, and are facing the downstairs fireplace. Maryot, pleased that he has his whole family herded together in one spot, is lying pressed against my right leg, between me and the fireplace. I can just see his big lanky body out of the corner of my eye.

Our conversation is suddenly interrupted by the sound of footsteps coming down the stairs. Tom and Kevin turn around to look behind themselves, as Rick and I look up to see the stairway. I can see Maryot's big head come up off his paws, and point to the top of the stairs....where nobody visible is making quite a ruckus, coming down to join us!

We all freeze. This is the first time we are all together to witness the spook. What had captured our attention was the unmistakable sound of feet descending the stairs, and the brightly lighted, clear sight of nobody there. None of us even breathes.

As the sound of the steps comes downward, I can see Maryot's long nose following the sound, lower and lower on the staircase.

When the invisible feet reach the bottom of the steps, they are then moving over a slab of concrete, with a heavy layer of carpeting on top of it. So, the sound of the footsteps stops the minute they hit the change in surface.

But Maryot's nose does not stop. It continues to follow a path that goes right through the middle of the circle the family forms in the room, and over to the fireplace at the far side of us. In order to continue tracking whatever it is that just walked through the middle of the family, Maryot has to swivel his head about three quarters of the way around. And that is exactly what he does.

Then he stares for a long moment at the fireplace, gives a big sigh, and lowers his head onto his paws again, quite content that all is as expected in his world.

By this time, all four of Maryot's people start speaking at once! "Wow!" "I told you there is a spook in this house!" "Who the heck....?" "Did you hear what I just heard?"

But Maryot remains the only one who, apparently, saw what he saw in addition to hearing what we all heard. And Maryot is not talking about what he saw.

Vision of White Light

By this point in our lives, Tom and I have been to a lecture on healing, I have joined an Edgar Cayce meditation group, and Tom and I often meditate together in the evening. One particular night's meditation session starts the way they usually do.

We have evolved an easy pattern. Tom lies on our bed, and I kneel beside him. Both of us are still completely clothed. We start meditating, and I just allow my hands to lightly skim an inch or so over his body. He might murmur something from time to time, which I lightly acknowledge with another murmur; I am grateful for the feedback.

His comments amaze me. He says: "Your hands are so hot." Or "How do you know where the places are that hurt? You go right to them, every time!"

21

I usually don't answer him at the time, and afterward, as we talk about a particular session, I can't give him a real answer. I don't know where he hurts, but my hands do. I just empty my mind and meditate for his healing. My hands find those places on their own.

I always start with a prayer—for protection, for us both. We both take these times together to be something very special, something almost sacred.

One evening Tom is in a lot of pain and asks if we can meditate. I settle into my usual routine, just kneeling quietly, allowing my breathing to slow down. I have no idea how long we are together like that… it may have been a half hour, or perhaps only ten to fifteen minutes.

Tom speaks quietly, then slightly louder, and more insistently: "Oh look! Look at the light! It is so beautiful… swirling… It's getting brighter!"

I open my eyes slightly to see what he is seeing, but I see nothing except that he has a radiant look on his face. And he is quietly crying. I close my eyes again, realizing he is having a meditation experience that I am not truly part of. So, I continue my own meditation, gently passing my hands over his torso, reaching under his back to the spot where my hands are led, and continuing until my hands cool off of their own accord.

I move from kneeling next to Tom to lying beside him on the bed. His face is still streaked with tears, and it still has that radiant look. I lay beside him quietly and wait until he is ready to talk.

Bit by bit, he shares his experience with me, thanking me profusely for something I knew I had neither done nor seen. I only saw his reaction. He tells me that tonight instead of thinking about his own health, he was praying for an old high school friend who he had just learned has cancer.

In his meditation, he saw a vision of what he called the White Light. At first it had been faint and seemed far away, but it got closer and brighter until he felt completely enclosed in its warmth. "It was Love, Rosey, the purest, purest Love!"

He is surprised that I did not see it. How could that be? But I had not. I had only seen its beauty reflected on his face.

As he insists that I helped channel it to him, I keep feeling that simply cannot be true: I wouldn't have any idea how to do such a thing. The only thing that I might have done was keep faith with the saying from the Bible: "Where two or more are gathered in My Name, there I will be, also."

The experience changes Tom. He is gentler, quieter, more thoughtful. We still laugh and joke together, disagree occasionally about some of the minor daily problems, but he is much more likely to reach over and touch my hand, or kiss the back of my neck as I am cooking supper, or find other little ways to show his love.

Shortly after that session, again while meditating with Tom, this blessing for him comes to me:

May the White Light always be with you,

May you feel your angels near you,

May you always have a dream.

A Blessing for the Teacher

I am in a beautiful, light-filled space of clear blue sky with a few fluffy white clouds. Just enough clouds to identify that the blue is really sky. At right angles to each other, two rows of tall Grecian columns meet, somewhat defining the space I am in. One row of columns is in front, the other to the right side. And, although I can see between the columns, they form the only "walls" of what is my classroom.

I am not alone: I am teaching a class, with each pupil occupying a space in carefully arrayed rows. The rows and columns of this class are all arranged like the desks in a traditional classroom. This is not at all like my real classroom, where the children cluster in skill-related groups, and I circulate among the groups.

This beautiful class in my dream is composed of souls, each one floating lightly in space, each one contained in a luminescent bubble. The bubbles have the beautiful swirling colors of a drop of oil on water. I move lightly between the rows, gently encouraging the inhabitant of each bubble as it prepares for... what? There is an air of excitement, as if they are getting ready for a special event. We all know what they are preparing for, but returning from my dream, I cannot remember what it is.

I tend to them without needing to speak. They can perceive my intentions, as well as the love I hold for each. And the love is returned.

My attention is drawn to the long row of Grecian columns in front of the class, and when I look up, I realize that there are two figures standing there observing my class. I know these beings, and hold them in high esteem. So, I automatically send them love as I look at them.

One of them nods to acknowledge my unspoken greeting. As he returns it, he includes a thought: "Well pleased." I gratefully accept his blessing, delighted he is pleased with the work I am doing with the class.

I wake from this dream in a state of calm, feeling loved, and I wonder: Is this what I will be able to do once I return Home? What are the souls preparing for? A new life on the planet? And the beautiful bubbles —are those the auras that some say surround us when we are on the earth?

The beauty of the light, the beauty of each soul as it shimmers in the light, and the palpable love we share, remain with me and inspire my daily work as an elementary school teacher. I am, indeed, very blessed.

Terrifying Vision of Trouble

There has been a period of several months where Tom has become convinced that he has to move to Newport, and I have a dream journal full of dreams that are screaming at me that I cannot give up my job, sell my house, uproot my sons from school, and move with him.

We wrestle with the problem daily, and finally come to the conclusion that he will go alone. The only other thing I know beside the fact that I cannot move with him is that I love him more than I have loved anyone in this life time. He is my beloved soul mate.

Since I have been with Tom, I have grown more than I had at any comparable period in my life. And I became a far better person because of his love. But my dreams are totally clear: I cannot move with him! So, I can only treat our pending separation with gentle care, and send him on his way.

We agree to get together often; then he moves out.

Neither of us has much money, so we seldom call each other, but we write often. Each of his long letters contains his surprise about the degree to which he misses me, and how much he feels we are still together even though we have a three-hour drive separating us.

I continue my daily meditations for him, with some remarkable results. One night he does call, asking if I have been thinking about him that day. I tell him that I had meditated for him, and felt a deep sense of peace. Then he tells me exactly what time it was when I had meditated! He is certain my energy reached and revitalized him; so certain that he checked the time so he could tell me what time I had sat in meditation.

With that kind of encouragement, I continue to meditate for Tom, sometimes more than once in a day. At times I sit in meditation just because I am lonely, and end up feeling connected to him and refreshed by his love.

One evening my meditation is particularly deep. As I sit in the stillness, I focus on my breath, letting feelings or phrases come and go with each inhale and exhale. While I have heard spoken words fairly often, I didn't usually have visual images. Tonight is different.

Faintly at first, I see the face of a person I recognize, but do not know well. 'George' had taught a class that Tom and I had attended where we attempted astral projection and past life regression. He also did some brief

25

psychic readings for class members, including one for Tom. The two men seemed to hit it off from the start.

George tells Tom that there is something very irregular about the place where Tom lives. George was making strong diagonal gestures with his hands while trying to describe it. He can't place the type of structure, but feels very strongly that it is there. Tom and I shrug, as his description does not match anything around our house.

When we get home late that night and drive into the driveway, the car lights shine on the back yard. Tom yells "Look!" and turns the lights on bright. While we had been gone that day, my sons had started some chores: they had dismantled an old deck to the swimming pool that we are going to remove, but they had done only half the job. They left a huge pile of lumber, piled on diagonal lines, just where the pieces had fallen when whacked with their sledge hammers.

So, George's diagonals are there... right in our back yard, although neither Tom nor I had seen them before the reading with George that night. It is spooky, and suggests that George has considerable psychic ability.

So, Tom continues his association with George, and I continue my meditations for Tom.

Months later, while I am meditating quietly, George's face appears in front of me. Then, in absolute horror, I realize that his curly hair is half-hiding short, curving devil's horns! I am looking at the devil! My eyes snap open, and with a sigh of relief, I realize that I am alone in my bedroom... that it is "only an image," no matter how frightening.

I pick up a book, to try to calm myself down, but the words go out of focus as I keep returning to the vision. What does it mean? Should I tell Tom what I saw? What can he do about it? What should he do about it?

With great relief I find a passage in my book about meditation that states that information received in meditation is provided in symbolic language. Because it cannot provide the direct information "this person is bad for you" the mind concocts a mental image of something that is bad... or bad for you.

Certainly adding "devil's horns" to a face I recognize gets that message across!

On Tom's next visit home, I tell him about the image. He is grave while I talk about the vision, listening closely, and then obviously relaxing when I tell him the explanation for the vision suggested by my book.

With a deep breath, he takes it in, and reaches over to hug me close. He hears me, and decides what to do with the information. I feel a huge sense of connection and relief. I have shared that troubling vision, without pretending to really know what it meant… but he is able to understand it in those terms, and accept it. He decides not to see George again.

I Can't Go to Newport

Tom and I make endless trips to Newport after he decides that he has to live there. He had an uncanny sense of familiarity with the town from his very first visit—an ongoing sense of deja vu. We've looked into the schools for the boys (they look dreadful), job possibilities for me (scarce to none), housing (we found a wonderful little chapel downtown that was for sale, but it would have been a budget-buster).

So, we make the trips down from my place in Massachusetts and then come home afterward to talk over what we've found. In the meantime, my nights are full of dreams. One dream after another tells me I cannot move down to Newport with Tom. I don't like that message, so I keep asking for more clarity from my dreams. I finally get it.

I dream that I am walking alone in a beautiful country, full of lush growth, and lots of beautiful, low stone fences. I am walking with Maryot, Tom's beloved German Shepard, who I suddenly realize is missing. I retrace my steps, calling out to him. I am gripped with fear by his absence. Then I hear his whining and barking, but he sounds strange.

I discover that the sounds are coming from a deep well, about five feet across, built of the same stones that are in the fences everywhere. The water level is below my reach, and Maryot has fallen in and can't get out!

In the process of trying to get him out, I fall in! And once I am in the well, he keeps pawing at me, and pushing me under the water. The water is deep, crystal clear, and cold. It is horrifying because Maryot's big paws keep me under the water, no matter how hard I struggle!

I wake in a cold sweat, sobbing. Of course, Maryot represents Tom in the dream. I have no clue why Tom would be "drowning" or would "pull me under with him" but I do know that I have a home and a job up in Massachusetts and the boys are more or less settled into a fairly good school. That dream is the final answer to whether I can pull up roots and join Tom in Newport. It cannot have been clearer: I cannot go!

Tom holds me in his arms as I relate the dream, and kisses the tears off my face. But he knows that I will have to listen to that dream, and I know it, too. He is going to follow his dream of being a marine photographer in Newport, and I am going to stay where I am. It is heart-breaking.

Trying to work out my feelings, I write Tom a letter:

My Darling Tom,

If we must part, I would like to part in peace; to be straight with each other; and to leave a door open to the future.

There are so many alternatives; if that special life that we have shared can no longer be, we do not need to be emotionally violent about its ending.

We can treat the relationship with all the respect we would treat a dear friend from whom we must part. Or as if the relationship were sick, or having been sick, was recovering. Or as if it were dying, but still dear to our hearts, although we can no longer relate to it daily.

With a sad heart, but with all my love,

Rosey

Now, at this point in my life I have never used the metaphor of dying. Why would I? We are in our 30's and nothing if not high-energy, full-of-life people! Creative, hard-working, laughing, dancing, loving; it is a wonderful life and we are living it to the fullest! But the metaphor that came unbidden in that letter warns of things to come.

2 Something in the Universe Knows My Name

I go about my daily life totally unprepared for what turns up during time I spend in the Alpha state. Dreaming and meditating produce fascinating and sometimes frightening things with amazing frequency!

An Innocent in a Distant Land

I have been meditating a lot lately. At least once a day I sit in individual meditation, I meet weekly with an Edgar Cayce Meditation group, and several times a week I meditate with Tom for healing.

Tom's gut is in a chronic state of uproar. His body plagues him with intermittent diarrhea that limits his life in many ways. It flares up whenever he is engaged in something stressful (like our first date), and leaves him with that dreadful feeling of no energy when his acids and salts are out of balance and he is dehydrated.

So, we meditate for healing. We attend a wonderful presentation by Olga Worrell, an internationally known spiritual healer. After her talk, we are introduced to her. When she shakes my hand she says: "You have healing hands, my dear. Are you aware of it?" Of course I wasn't. I hadn't even heard of such a thing until I had listened to her speech that evening. But I am eager to learn if I can help my beloved Tom get well.

One evening, on a happy emotional high from a successful week of prayer and meditation, I settle in to meditate alone. I go into an alpha state so often I can drop pretty deeply, pretty quickly. On the way down this particular night, I muse that Edgar Cayce's ability to see the Akashic Records is fascinating, and I would love to understand that kind of knowledge about the universe.

So, I drop deeper into meditation, totally at peace in the safety and quiet of my bedroom. Not long afterward, less than a foot in front of my face, I hear a woman's voice quietly say "Rosemary?"

I snap out of my Alpha state, open my eyes, and practically shout: "Who knows my name?"

And then I laugh at my silly self. All bravado, I want to learn the universe's secrets and be allowed to read the Akashic records, but it is far too personal if someone in the universe knows my name!

It takes me almost a week before I can meditate again. That event was far too vivid, and I am suddenly aware that there really is something "out there" that I can reach, and touch, and it can touch me back. This is a very serious matter that I have to understand and respect.

The Camp Fire Burns So Brightly

I'm in an Edgar Cayce "Search for God" meditation group. It is an atypical group, from what I hear, in that it is made up mostly of men: there are eight men and two women, including me. We meet at the home of the other woman and her partner.

It is a lovely group of people, soft spoken, interested in following the discipline of doing a daily meditation, intent on the Bible study that is part of the Edgar Cayce study program, and willing to pray for and with each other. It is an atmosphere that I really like.

It is hard to meditate daily. Being a teacher and a single mother of teenage sons makes just getting through the day (and my 50-mile round-trip to work) about all I can manage some days. But I keep trying to meditate daily, and am pleased when I succeed. There is something deeply familiar about the meditative state, but I can't quite figure out what it is. I really like it… it is so refreshing and uplifting.

I have been a member of the Cayce group for about six weeks now, and the pattern of what we do in the Search for God group is becoming familiar. I find myself really looking forward to meeting with them. And meditating in the group seems more powerful than when I'm meditating alone at home. I keep forgetting to ask about that.

Tonight's meditation in group is deep and powerful. When the timer goes off in the other room and we start to come out of the meditation, one of the men to my left stretches lightly and quietly says "The camp fire was really burning brightly tonight."

A couple of the other members of the group smile in agreement. But we are sitting on the carpet in the living room, not around a camp fire, and the statement doesn't make sense! I ask what he means. He explains that the group has sometimes experienced a sense of a burning light that hovers in the middle of their circle. They have dubbed it "the camp fire."

My eyes open wide with wonder, as I blurt out "I saw that! You're right! There was a bright light, right in the middle of our circle! I could see the brightness, even with my eyes closed! But there is no lamp or candle there, much less a camp fire! Where does the light come from?"

Knowing smiles are all I get for an answer. And the somewhat cryptic explanation that this phenomenon has occurred multiple times in the group. When I ask what the source could be, the guys give a slight shrug of their shoulders. I feel like the kid whose adults are evading her questions about adult things. It is a little frustrating to me, but done with no ill will… just an attitude of "It's OK. You'll find out in due time."

But that stunning sensation of a brilliant light, when there is no physical source for it in the room, pushes me to study more about meditation. And it keeps me returning to deeper levels of meditation as the "discipline" of meditating changes into an anticipated daily pleasure. A source of calm. A place to go for understanding of the dilemmas in my life. A refuge, when just doing the dailies gets too much to bear.

I Came to Help You Know

"I came to help you know."

Your words came in the dark,

at night; in sleep?

There was no vision?

no dream remembrance?

that came with them

and you were sleeping

when I responded to your voice.

Were your subconscious and mine
so closely tuned that we could speak
in some pure way and
by-pass the conscious state?

At any rate,
you came to help me know.
Once we both knew that,
you left.

Thank you for your visit.
Thank you for caring enough to come.
Thank you for sharing yourself with me.
And may the deepest blessings
that God holds in his richness
go with you
as you go
your way.

I wrote that poem in my dream journal, dated it, and made a copy for
Tom. Four months and eight days after I had this dream, Tom died of cancer.

Farewell to Newport

It is over. The long days and nights of vigil as Tom lay dying in the hospital, the Memorial service for him, cleaning out his apartment. We're done, at last. I'm grateful for the closeness Tom's family and I share, and marvel that we have been able to work through so many difficult issues without ever getting short tempered with each other. His folks are so loving; I feel deeply blessed, despite the huge pain of losing Tom.

As I drive from downtown Newport towards the highway back up to Massachusetts and home, I pass the large roadside sign that announces I'm leaving Newport and thanks me for my visit. I'm suddenly struck with the enormity of what that visit has included, and get all teary-eyed with sentimentality.

At that instance, a large gull flies right over my windshield and plops a huge deposit directly in front of my vision! I can almost hear Tom's voice: "Cue the gulls!" I break up laughing. That has all the mischievousness that he would have brought to the event, for sure!

Tom Comes Back to Visit

Tom visits me after he died! I have been grieving deeply. Because I have no choice, I have returned to my job. I try not to cry in front of my own kids. But to keep from exploding with grief, I cry every time I'm alone in the car, then stop the tears moments before I arrive at my destination.

I can't stand to listen to music of any kind. Happy music is grossly inappropriate, sad music only adds fuel to my intense, gut-wrenching pain.

Nighttime is the worst. Mostly I make it through by praying for Tom, for Kevin, Rick, and myself, and for Tom's folks. I eventually fall asleep. I can't meditate. Tom and I have been there together in so much beauty, and in order to meditate, I would have to drop that shell of protection I've erected to distance myself from my own emotions. And that is just too much to ask.

Then Tom comes to visit. It is still clear, 50 years later, without reference to my dream journal.

I dream he is at my house with his father and me. All three of us know that he is dead, but he is there, and that is fine. He is also my handsome Tom again, not the horrid, gaunt skeleton that the cancer had reduced him to before it finally released him and let him die. I am stunned that that skeleton is gone, and there is my Tom in his casual slacks and a plaid sports shirt, looking strong, healthy, and happy.

The three of us start "putting my house in order." Even in my dream, I smile at the pun of these two men helping me house-clean, while we all understand the deeper significance of the words and the act.

Tom and I don't need to talk. We communicate by just thinking our thoughts; the other person is somehow able to understand them. Effortless and amazing, but puzzling! He can hear my thoughts without my deciding to speak them... I don't know what to do with that loss of privacy!

I am struck with wonderment. I wonder how he is, and immediately know the answer??he is perfect. He is not just "well," or "fine," or "without pain." He is, of essence, perfect.

It is breathtaking to see the handsome, vibrant Tom I have loved with, and danced with, and sailed with, not the pathetic shadow to which the cancer reduced his body at the end. After the horror of watching him die of cancer, seeing him well, strong, and perfect again fills me with joy and wonder.

I want to ask how he spends his time, but I get tangled up on how to word my question. Is there a sense of time in "eternity?" Can I ask how he "spends his days?" Does eternity have distinct days? While I frantically think of a different way to phrase my question, Tom's smile keeps getting bigger and bigger. I suddenly remember that he can hear the mental gymnastics I am going through, so I finally just blurt out "How do you spend your time?"

His gentle response: "We are busy—learning all the time, working on projects—you are going to love it, Rosey!"

I love his answer, but I ache in my aloneness, so I blurt out: "But I miss you so much!"

"You don't need to! I am right here, with you, all the time."

I don't understand how that statement can be, but seeing him whole again takes away all my pain and fear, and leaves me light and glowing with joy. I wonder if we can touch. He smiles the famous Tom smile, and puts his long arms around me as I stretch up to return his hug.

Then I just lay in bed luxuriating in the warmth of love returned, of love that transcends time and death, and of the deep physical knowing that I have just been held in love.

The Call of the Bell

I am lying on my energy worker's massage table, as she quietly does her bodywork magic: some Reiki, some Polarity, whichever of the eight healing modalities that she has mastered that she thinks my body needs at the moment. Possibly near trance, certainly in an Alpha state, I am quietly talking about some of the past lives I'm sure I've lived, and how I know. It's really quite clear.

I was a ballerina once. From the very first time I saw someone dance, I knew I could do that. No, that's not right! I knew I had done that! My bones know how to dance, deep down. They know the joy and they know the pain. They can leap, pause on the cusp of the up-beat, and breathe the music. They know the discipline. They know the love. I have not danced professionally in this lifetime, but my dance card was always full when I was in school. I attracted male dancers like a butterfly attracts its mate.

On my first date with Tom, the instant I step into his arms to dance, I know I am home! I feel his aura fold around me and hold me in love. I feel his joyful, vibrant energy surround me, and invite me to join it in exploration of wonders! Yes, I understand about good old sexual attraction, but this is fundamentally different. It is all of that, but it is specifically welcoming me back to his special energy, his way of seeing things and doing things, his way of being in the world. And it is magical!

From the first time that I saw Haiku poetry, I knew I had read, or heard, or written thousands of lines of it. Ages worth of seventeen-syllable thoughts, spun out to glisten.

A haiku spontaneously comes to me while I'm lying on the table:

Dew on spider's web.

Sudden breezes set it free.

Lost joy, lost delight.

As a part of a Comparative Religion class in college; Zen Buddhism was required reading. But it was with the wonder of recognition, that I re-read lines lived close to my heart, for ages. I felt the mystical riddles tug at my soul and whisper "Here! Come! Here lies the mystery."

I tell my Reiki worker that I had heard a Buddhist bell months ago, and it resonated deep to my core with its purity of tone. "How does it work?" I muse: "By definition, resting a bell on a cushion should muffle the tone, but that is the way the Buddhist bell is rung..."

She says she has such a bell, and we can listen to it once we are done with the session. So, as I put on my shoes, she returns to the room, and strikes the bell softly.

The bell is brass. The sound, shimmering crystal gold. My insides resonate to its tone, and tears stream down my cheeks, washing the rapturous smile evoked by that deeply familiar sound.

"Would you like to strike it?" Frances asks. "You can, you know."

Startled, I look up at her. "No! I am not worthy to ring the bell."

"Oh, yes you are," she says firmly as she hands me the soft cushion, the perfectly formed bowl on top, with its reed-wrapped clapper.

I strike it once. Too tentatively; it doesn't sing. So, I strike it again. Just so! With a light wrist, but firm, as a dancer dances, or musician plays, or a monk rings the holy bell.

As more tears come, I lean back in my chair, cradling the bell, cherishing the sound. Francis quietly says "It is the Call to Meditation."

Dream of Coding Errors

From time to time my dreams prompt me to do something specific or provide very specific information. The problem is knowing when to trust that the data is valid and when to try to interpret the dream by understanding it is a metaphor of some type. One that turned out to be startlingly true gets me really interested in reading about dreams and learning how to harness their fabulous power.

I am transitioning from being a teacher to working as an editor. My first editing job is with a company that publishes the basal readers used in public schools. Next, I am able to parlay the skills I learned there to a job editing in a small computer company. The learning curve is pretty steep, but computer companies seem to be places where one can earn a really good salary and do interesting work, so I am excited about getting up to speed in my new job.

As an editor, I negotiate with the writer about changes for grammar or consistency of terminology. In addition, I input the hundreds of the equivalent of HTML codes to turn plain computer text into printed type. Once I release a book it goes to the publisher electronically and comes back as galleys, ready for the last proofing before being printed in hundreds of copies.

Throughout all the editing stages, I am working blind. I cannot see the effects that the codes which I input have on the text until I see the actual galleys. Then, for the first time, I can see the type as it will appear, with different sizes of type for headings, and bold or Italics added for emphasis. For the first time tables appear, as do numbered steps, and bulleted lists. Making corrections to galleys comes with a heavy cost. Even a tiny change, such as deleting a punctuation mark, is tallied up, and it is charged to whomever ordered the change: the editorial department or the writer.

I read and re-read the 20 files' worth of text endlessly, making sure that the syntax for the codes is entered exactly right.

My drop-dead date when it has to be shipped to the publisher is one day away, when I have a dream that feels so real that I wake up laughing. I know immediately that this dream is totally realistic, and I also know I would barely have time to prevent an enormous, costly mistake. One so big it could easily make me lose my job!

Every file that makes up the book has to open with a paragraph consisting of nothing but codes that establish the font family, default type size, sizes for all levels of headings, and so forth. My dream warns me that those paragraphs are missing from some of the 20-plus files in the book. The result would be that none of the type from those files would be correct, and dozens of whole pages would have to be re-set and a whole new group of galleys ordered. There could easily be fifty pages of trashed copy! Knowing that they charge to change a single comma, I can't imagine what would be charged for fifty pages!

It is only 4:00 AM, but I quickly get ready for work, and drive to the office. Because we editors frequently work late, I have a key to the door, so I let myself in, turn on the lights, and settle in to check every file for its opening definitions paragraph.

Sure enough, starting with the seventh file, I am missing that definitions paragraph in every single file. That makes a total of sixteen files where every single letter of text would be completely wrong... an unimaginably colossal error!

Just as I am finishing my whole set of corrections, the rest of the department is coming in to start work. When I try to tell them why I am working so hard so early in the morning, they just look at me like I am from another planet: what do you mean you dreamed that the files had errors in them, and the dream was accurate?

At the end of that wonderful day I stop at my favorite book store and buy a book on the power of dreams, and how to interpret them. And I buy a beautiful dream journal to record my dreams in. It feels like the perfect way to celebrate my dream life!

Zapped!

I am lying on my Polarity Therapist's massage table, receiving an energy healing session. These sessions have a familiar pattern that my body really seems to need: I lie, fully clothed, while she gently touches different parts of my body. I usually allow myself to drift into an Alpha state.

On this evening, I let myself drift in and out of Alpha, talking from time to time about some memory that has come to the surface, or some relationship issue.

She slowly works around my body, usually starting with my ankles, then moving up one side and eventually going to the other side. She just touches a point and gently rocks her hands on it. If it is my knee, my whole leg may jiggle a bit, but there is no real pressure being exerted, as might happen in massage. Just a light touch.

On this night she has started work on my left leg and has gotten up to my knee. Still touching my left knee, she reaches diagonally across my body and lightly makes contact with her other hand to my right shoulder.

Zap!

The electrical spark makes enough sound and sizzles both our bodies enough so we know it has happened. My eyes open in surprise as she says: "What was that?"

It felt just like the small spark you can get if you have shuffled across a carpet in the winter and then touch somebody else, or touch an electrical appliance. Just a small discharge of electrical energy.

But there is a problem with that simple answer. She was already in contact with my body, so she should have already been grounded, relative to my (or her own) electric field. When your touch sparks off somebody else it can only happen once, the first time that you touch them.

So, what caused this spark? Could she have made a connection between different electrical circuits in my body? Acupuncture, acupressure, and several other healing modalities are effective because they utilize a system of energy pathways that exist in the body. This spark certainly seemed like a verification that these pathways are not just metaphors.

You Better Go Slow

For a week I've been in a state of panic. I have decided that I want to become an energy healer. I feel so much better after receiving a session that I feel certain I am supposed to become a therapist in this field. So, I am about to apply for the three-year training cycle. It's going to be very expensive and require that I devote all my vacation time to the project, but that feels right. After a few phone calls to headquarters I learn that the next step is for me to send an email stating why I want to learn how to do body work.

I can't write the email. I have no idea why, but I can't. I'm paralyzed, frozen.

The sponsoring organization for this type of body work has scheduled a nearby weekend retreat and I receive a notice so I can sign up for it. But when the schedule arrives, I'm thrilled at first, then I panic.

I can't fill out the simple form to register for the weekend's classes.

I am paralyzed! My insides are screaming: "I can't do this!" But I also want it as much as anything I have wanted for years. And I'm totally confused by not being able to sign up for either the weekend retreat or the three-year program.

I meditate about this, I talk with my body worker and everyone else I know, but I remain blocked, and I cannot complete the application process.

Days slip by and I have another appointment with my healer. I state my intention for the session: I want to learn why I can't apply to become a healer myself. And I want to eliminate that block… so I can write the silly emails and fill out the applications.

We work diligently on this for the entire session, and deal with the huge issues I have about becoming a healer. I've tried to follow this path before, with Tom, and although he felt he had a spiritual healing, he died. My skeptical brain feels it would be arrogant of me to believe that I could heal him, but I also know that others have been healed spiritually and physically. Why couldn't he have received a physical healing?

Tom and I were working on healing alone. I had no formal training and no support system. Surely with a formal program and a teacher I could learn what I had done wrong, and learn how to do it better?

As I leave the session, I feel centered, sure that I really want this, and ready to go home and apply. All the way home I concentrate on writing the email in my mind and completing the application. As I drive the words form in my mind, crystal clear in intent.

On the route home there is a stretch of roadway where the town has been replacing underground water pipes, and the road has been torn up for months on end. Tonight, as I ease into the bumpy construction area, I see an enormous sign, hand painted with International Orange spray paint. It reads:

"YOU BETTER GO SLOW!"

First, I laugh out loud, thinking "Some poor slob bumped over this impossible road surface too fast and tore the bottom out of his car!" Then I hit the brakes so hard I almost throw myself against the steering wheel despite my seat belt. What did that sign say?

I am currently in the middle of reading Sacred Contracts by Carolyn Myss, which describes how to use synchronicity to find your spiritual path:

What do I believe my spiritual path is?

Working for healing.

What was I thinking about when I saw this sign?

Becoming a healer in one particular school.

And what is this particular piece of synchronicity telling me?

R-i-g-h-t!

45

So instead of going home and dashing off an email describing how sure I am that I am supposed to become a healer, I write that part of the email, and then try to explain the mind-boggling message in the sign.

I can't send the email. It reads like I have totally lost my mind.

By now it is way past my bedtime, and tomorrow is a work day, so I decide to sleep on it, and request guidance from my dreams. The next morning, I wake early but I am only clear about one thing: I don't believe I really saw that sign, or that it really said what I thought it said. The guidance is far too bald (surely synchronicity is at least subtle?). I have to see the sign again.

I hurry through my morning shower, pack my digital camera, and head for that construction site, determined to get a photo of the sign.

Success! It is a beautiful sunny morning, and there is the sign, leaning against a telephone pole. It is even brighter orange than I remembered, and bigger. The telephone pole gives it some scale: it is easily three times wider than the pole it is leaning on! Big!

I take the photograph and head for work. I print out the sign on a full-sized piece of paper, and it is gloriously clear! Then I decide I need to carry it around with me a while. So I shrink the image, make a couple printouts that are only two inches in each direction, cover them with clear plastic so they have some strength, and pop one in my pocket. I need to have my fingers find it, and hold it, and ponder its mystery until I can understand it. I walk around with it in my pocket all day, prompting my mind to find clarity every time I touch it.

The next night I have to pass over the construction site again. I am looking for the telephone pole with the sign when I realize that I am at the place where it had been and it is gone! So, it only existed in that format, at that spot where I would drive by it, for less than 24 hours! During the 24-hour period when I was trying to write the application to become a healer! And still there the next morning when I needed the certainty that can only come from the objective record of a photograph! That sign's appearance is pretty much custom-made synchronicity, if you ask me! I can't help but laugh about it, but it also makes me want to cry!

Experience with the nasty outcomes that seem to occur when I ignore such blatant messages from the Universe leads me to cancel my application to the school.

I feel heart-wrenchingly sad. Why can't I become a healer?

I have come to call the sign "My billboard." I don't have a clue why it is delivering that particular message. I just feel I have to honor its presence in my life. I am grateful that I took its portrait, as that is all I have to go on from its brief existence in my life. I carry the picture of it in my pocket daily, still pondering its message, still unclear why it had to be that way.

Postscript

Two months later, the reason for my billboard's message becomes clear: I am laid off at work, so the job and the salary that would have supported three years of training have suddenly disappeared. The economy is in bad shape, and I am unable to find work for over six months. And when I do find work again, it is as a contractor. Contractors are paid by the hour; you don't get vacations, and you can't take time off to attend week-long seminars on a regular basis.

Thank you, Universe, for making my billboard so big, so International Orange, so blatantly clear! I did not want to believe it when I saw it, but I would be in a nasty financial situation if I had not heeded it.

It is clear that becoming a healer is not my path. I can't afford the course of study, now that I have lost my job, and the Universe is being unrelentingly clear that I am not supposed to pursue this. I have to listen when the Universe gives me billboards like the one it created to tell me You Better Go Slow.

Tonight's meditation is on this impossibly confusing juncture I have reached: If I am not supposed to do that work, what am I supposed to do? Why am I on the planet? Surely there is a path for me somewhere?

Answers don't always come quickly, but the months of preparation for that decision pay off, and my answer comes so clearly it is astounding that I had not seen it before: I should work in Hospice! I have lost two partners to cancer, I have survived cancer myself, and I had a beautiful meditation when going into my own cancer surgery. Together, they left me knowing that I am not afraid of death! How could I be better prepared for Hospice work than that?

I test the idea with those who know me best, and get huge support for this plan. This is the area where all my skills could be brought to bear. In fact, an area where the nudging that I sometimes get from the Universe may best be heard and put to use. Thank you, Angels!

I locate a Hospice center near me, easily fill out the application for the training course for Volunteers, and start my journey on a new path.

A Christmas Gift while Driving on Ice

It is Christmas Day; Tom died just last October. With my sons help, I have somehow decorated the house, and bought and wrapped Christmas presents for the huge number of people on my lists. On Christmas morning my boys and I open our presents for each other, eat our annual steak and eggs Christmas breakfast, and leave for the airport. After I put them on the plane to be with their father, I will go over to Tom's parents' house to be with them and open more presents. I am numb, but functioning, and have worked hard to make a good Christmas morning for my sons.

At 17 and 13, Rick and Kevin are experienced flyers, and the Christmas day flight down to their father in New Jersey is apparently one of their more enjoyable trips. The plane is usually virtually empty, and the stewardesses give two teenagers traveling alone a lot of attention. I know they are fighting sadness, too. But they are coping and I'm sure they look forward to some Christmastime happiness while they are with their father.

As soon as they are called to board, I hug them and quickly walk away, allowing tears to pour down my face for the first time that day. The plane gets off just before the pending storm. The day wears the falling barometer and overcast skies like a shroud. The weather is a perfect match for my mood: I feel the pressure of desperately needing to weep on a day when we are supposed to be festive.

I allow the tears to come unchecked as I drive to see Tom's parents. Hopefully, that will release enough pressure to get me through the rest of the day.

It works for the most part. In our shared grief, his parents and I exchange the tokens of love we have bought for each other, talk about how it is hard to find the spirit to celebrate, and comfort whoever needs it at any particular moment.

By mid-afternoon, the storm has arrived, and I leave for home. I am dreading being alone, but the weather forecast says the storm will be heavier as the day goes on, so I don't want to postpone the trip too long.

The roads start to ice up, but my big station wagon is heavy and very stable. And since I have put more than 150,000 miles on it, I know how to keep it on a steady track. I keep a slow, steady pace and try to stay aware of whether the wheels are grabbing the road properly. Luckily, there are very few cars on the road.

Coming up ahead, I have a series of three sharp little hills to climb and there is a stop light at the top of the third and highest hill. I hold my breath hoping that the light lets me ease up the hill and over the top without having to stop while I am still on the steep slope.

But the light goes red as I start to climb that last hill. I ease off the gas pedal to try to keep moving just above the point where I would start skidding, but the strategy doesn't work. I get to the top of the hill but the light is still red, and I have to come to a complete stop.

But I can't! As soon as I stop moving forward, my car starts slipping backward, while still in gear and with my foot on the brake! My tires have absolutely no traction on the road at all! I put all my weight on the brake pedal, but only keep sliding backward!

Nobody is behind me on the roadway, but it is terrifying! I am not moving fast, but I have no control whatsoever, and am sliding directly backward, down hill! If a car crowns the hill coming at me from behind, they won't be able to stop either!

Then the light at the top of the hill ahead of me changes to green, and over the hill comes a stream of traffic, as totally out of control coming forward as I had been going backward. The hill is totally covered with ice, and they can't drive in a straight line. They skid down the hill all askew, and head my way as I hold my breath.

I have reached the bottom of the little valley by then, and my car has finally come to a stop. It is still on the roadway and now a half-dozen cars are skidding down the road toward me. When I check my rear-view mirror, I suddenly see more cars coming in towards us from the other direction.

I let out a cry to my angels for help, and brace myself for the crash as the cars plow into each other.

I hear crash after crash after crash. I am all hunched over, braced against the steering wheel, waiting for the jolt that means somebody hit me. But although the crashes continue, the jolt never comes! Then it is quiet.

I open my eyes and look into the face of a driver in another car who is barely inches from my face. His car has been hit in front by the cars coming down the hill toward us, and from behind by cars coming in the other direction, but it had not hit me. Nobody had been speeding, so none of the passengers have been hurt, but there are a dozen cars that I can see, and they are a mess. And we are all trapped on the highway, down in this little valley, waiting for another stream of cars to pile up against us!

Then I hear a siren. I just sit there, trying to calm down as a police officer walks among the cars, instructing each of the drivers what to do. The road surface is so slick, the officer can't stand or walk between the cars without bracing himself against them. The whole hillside is still a skating rink.

I roll down my window. "Who did you hit?" he demands.

"Nobody, Sir."

"NO?"

"No, Sir."

"Well then, who hit you?"

"Nobody, Sir!"

"W-h-a-t? You're in the middle of a 27-car pileup and nobody hit you?" He goes to check the other end of my car, to see if I am lying. Sure enough, I am untouched. He comes back to my window. "Then get out of here," he orders.

"I can't, Sir. I slid backwards down the hill, with my foot full against the brakes! I can't drive up it! I have to wait for the sand truck!"

"Get your car out of the way!" he growls.

"No Sir! If I try to drive forward, I'll skid into these other cars, and crush you between them!"

"I've got to get you out of here before any of these other drivers hears that you got off Scott free, or they'll kill you! Now git!"

He is yelling at me by this point. He braces himself against the car behind him and pushes my car to try to get it rolling. It does get just enough traction to move forward, and I inch up to where the sand truck has laid down a layer of salt and sand… and ease over the top of the hill, triumphant!

Thank you, Angels! A 27-car pileup, and I was protected in the midst of it! An extraordinary Christmas gift, indeed!

3 Getting it Together

Do you sometimes get a nudge to do something N.O.W.? No waiting! Move it! Get it done! Like, *move it!* And do you sometimes find out later that there was something serious behind that push? Right. I know about that.

Break In!

I live in a suburb of one of the large metropolitan areas in the Northeast. It is a pretty place, full of old brownstones... and I'm the lucky owner of one lovely brownstone and the inhabitant of its third-floor apartment. It takes me over a year to find it as my budget does not match the going rate for such a gem. And it is a rough-cut gem when I first find it: the third floor has no heat, no hot water, and one 15-amp fuse for the whole four rooms! Not to mention the 107-year old walls and ceilings full of cracks and patches. But ten months after I buy it, I have a lot of practice fixing horsehair plaster and all those other problems are history.

I'm a technical writer for a small computer start-up, and one of the perks of the job is that we get to work from home two days a week. Actually, when you count the hours we spend working on the weekends, we work from home four days a week. But by being provided with a complete personal computer, and a direct line into the downtown main computer, email, and so on, we do not have to "work late at the office" or go back into the office on the weekends. Nice!

It is a lovely spring morning, and I'm totally concentrating on a new chapter that has to be ready for its first review by the end of the week. The only distraction I have is that when I came home last night, I discovered that my old refrigerator had breathed its last, so I have to buy a new one today. No problem; I'll do that after I get this chapter sorted out, and need a break.

While deep in concentration, I hear a loud crash in the distance, and then a bunch of doggy barks, but this is a city I live in. There could be plenty of reasons for a crash. And I am determined to push this chapter along. Later on, there is another crash and more doggy barks, but again I don't let it break my concentration. It barely registers, except that I remember it later in the day, when I try to reconstruct when different events happened.

Mid-morning, I suddenly have the urgent feeling that I am being pushed to go find that fridge… now! I'm being pushed so hard I don't even shut down my computer. That is a real no-no, and they'll be mad in the office if they find out, but I'm suddenly in a huge hurry to go. So, I grab my pocketbook and keys, run galumping down the two long flights of stairs, and out to my car.

I finish my mission in the large box store, park out front of my house, and stride up the stairs to the front door. When I try to insert my front door key, the door swings open on its own! Darn those tenants, they must not have locked it. You can't do that in the city; we'll get broken into!

As soon as the door opens, the two dogs from the first and second floor apartments greet me as I step in. "What's this? A doggy convention? You guys aren't supposed to be out without your owners," I announce to the pups. I start to knock on the first-floor door, to tell the gal who lives there that her dog is loose, but that door also swings open when I knock. That startles me… and I gingerly stick my head in the apartment. I can see all the way to the back. There is nobody home, but the back door to the outside is wide open!

Suddenly I freeze! I realize that the tenants did not leave the doors open, the doors were broken open by somebody else! I back out of the apartment, my heart racing. I fly down the front steps and run to my car.

Now, this is in the days before cell phones, and I need to get to a phone booth to call 911! The officer at the police station tells me I should return home, and wait for the squad car to arrive. I decide to wait in my car out front of the building. No way am I going to go back in there alone!

It takes almost twenty minutes for the squad car to arrive, which frightens and aggravates me. But in the meantime, a nondescript, 30-something, white male comes from the back of the building with a large box in his hands. He puts the box into the back of his shiny, red and white Ford truck, gets in, and drives away. But I've never seen him in the neighborhood before, so I note the make of the truck, and its license number. I quickly write it down so I won't forget it.

When the police finally arrive, I get out of my car, and give them the limited amount of information I have. When we get to the front door, they say "You first." I look at them in horror, shaking my head no! They draw their guns and walk into the first-floor apartment. One officer points to the dead bolt on the door, which has a long piece of the wooden door jamb still attached. "He kicked it in!" he says, with no particular emphasis in his voice.

They call the name of the tenant, and move slowly into the apartment, asking me if it always looks like that. There are several big boxes, all packed up, sitting on the dining room table. I tell them about the man I saw get into his truck with another large box. I ask them to put out a police call for that shiny red and white Ford truck and read them the license plate number I wrote down.

"Lady, youze is hy-sterical! That's no license number for a truck. It's a number for a car!" And they refuse to notify any other police units of the identified truck. I protest that maybe he stole the plates off a car, but they won't listen to me. After all, I'm hysterical, right? Wrong! I'm plenty scared but I've been calmly feeding them the information they request.

They shut the back door of the apartment, and make their way up to the second floor, which is a repeat of the downstairs: the door has been kicked open, there is a big box on the dining room table, but nobody is in sight.

When they go up the stairs to my apartment on the third floor, I stay on the second floor landing. If the burglar is in my apartment, he cannot get out without walking right past us. The only other way out of my apartment is the fire escape, so he will be trapped there! Just as I would have been, if I had still been home and he broke in on me!

I breathe a huge sigh of relief when they find that my own front door is still securely locked. We go back to the second floor, where I insist that they check every nook and closet, and then go down the back stairway to be certain he is not lurking there. He is nowhere to be found, so finally they leave.

I start shaking and crying as I realize how close I had been to having him break in on me. When I had left to go refrigerator shopping, it almost was not my decision... some other power had practically picked me up by the scruff of my neck and shoved me out of the house!

Still crying, I sit on the stairs next to the first-floor apartment, with the tenants' two dogs who are trying their best to console me. Thank you, Angels! It is pretty obvious who or what had insisted I go shopping at that particular moment an hour or so ago!

I call my handyman, and ask him to come over and secure the broken doors. I call my two tenants, to tell them what has happened. Finally, I call a friend, and ask if I can stay overnight with him. I don't think I'll be able to sleep in my own apartment tonight.

Tom Gives His Approval

My moment by moment awareness every single day and night is that Tom has died. Our wonderful relationship has been shattered by the horror of this beautiful, gentle man turning into a skeleton in eight weeks of fruitless hospital care.

They say there are numerous different mental states people go through as they try to come to terms with their own mortality. Tom never shares the painful ones with me. He is just infallibly thrilled that I have made the three-hour drive to see him. He welcomes the little things I can do for him: the back rubs, the offers to get a basin and wash his hands and face, the trips in the wheelchair to the solarium, or to the tiny outside patio that is sheltered from the wind.

I have his family for support, and begin every trip into the hospital with a brief visit to the Chapel, where I ask for the strength to do whatever Tom needs most, and guidance to know what that is.

When I am away from him, I continue my regular regimen of meditating for his healing, and including him in my prayers. I have my sons, my job, and our home to take care of. While Tom is in the hospital, everything else except these major things gets put on hold.

After Tom dies, one of my other friends, a man whom I had dated before I met Tom, had been asking to take me out to dinner. He encourages me to talk and listens to the tales of Tom's last illness. I don't want to "date," but this person feels safe. We had all belonged to the same group of single adults, and Tom knew him. I know that Tom really disliked this guy, but that doesn't seem as if it should matter now.

Some long time after Tom has gone, one of these evenings together ends in a gentle invitation to bed. I accept, with the warning that I don't know what will happen: I might end up in tears. Not to worry, I am told.

What does happen is a good deal more startling than tears. We have gone through some gentle preliminaries, and are getting engrossed when I momentarily open my eyes and see Tom's face smiling from over this man's shoulder! Just Tom's face, with little wings beside it, like the baby cherubim that decorate some old-fashioned Valentine's cards. He is grinning and beaming in approval, as he vigorously shakes his head "Yes!"

I am flabbergasted! "Yes?" I ask, not realizing I'm speaking out loud.

"Yes!" But it is the voice of my partner for the evening, not Tom's voice, that answers. It takes more than a little while, and more than a few tears, to recover my equilibrium.

Another Prophetic Dream

After the break-in at my Somerville house, I cannot spend the night there again. Even though the break-in was during the day, I simply no longer feel safe in the building, and night times are worst.

Somehow, this suits my friend perfectly, and he invites me to move in with him. We have been talking about going to that next step in our relationship, so I am thrilled, but a bit surprised when he offers. I pack up my clothes and the things I need for my home office, and rent out my apartment, totally furnished, right down to the wash cloths and pillow cases.

This new relationship has somewhat of a bumpy start, but I feel that I learned so much about how to have a good relationship when I was with Tom, that it will only be a matter of time to straighten things out between my new partner and myself.

Part of the negotiations between us revolve around having an exclusive partnership. I have had my fill of part-time lovers during the early years of my divorce, and I want none of it. Especially now that we are living together. I am adamant and very clear about that. He keeps dodging making a promise, but he says he will try.

I feel like things are going well. He is a good cook, and he likes to cook. And I love coming home after a long day to a house that smells like good food. Supper is usually ready at the end of my hour's long commute, and that is wonderful!

He is so smart, and so funny, and I love our conversations. We are both interested in fine art and music. It is wonderful having company to go to concerts and to go to one of the great museums in our area.

As a very senior engineer who specializes in the interfaces between different types of systems, he works on contract with some well-known companies, on fascinating projects. But the work is not steady, and as each project ends, he spends a lot of time trying to land the next job.

One Saturday he is at a conference of engineers, hoping to network himself into another such project, so I know I have a long day alone ahead of me. It doesn't bother me, but I also do not have any projects of my own to do in his house. No curtains to make, or bathrooms to wallpaper. I realize that I don't yet feel completely "at home" in this house. But those things take time, so I shrug off the feeling, and dig into some work I brought home from the office.

After several hours of writing and editing, I feel sleepy, so I lay down to take a nap. I fall into a sleep that is deep enough to have a dream… and I wake up saying out loud: "Oh, no! Not again!" even though I don't remember the dream.

I get up and go straight downstairs to his office, pull open the top right-hand drawer of his desk, and there, as I knew from my dream it would be, is irrefutable evidence that he is not trying hard enough with the exclusivity clause in our agreement.

He loves expensive gadgets of every kind, including a Polaroid camera. Unlike regular cameras of the day, the Polaroid takes pictures that print out immediately. And because he always buys the top of the line, this one prints a time and date stamp right on the picture. So, these nude photos of some lady are date-stamped two days previously, while I was at work. I am furious!

I put the pictures away carefully, just as I had found them, and pour myself a cup of coffee to sit and think through what has just happened. I feel uncomfortable about having gone through his desk. But I didn't "go through it" on a random search. My dream told me exactly where to look: the top right-hand drawer of that desk, all the way at the back. I didn't even know what I was looking for, but I recognized it instantly when I saw it.

The evidence provided by the picture does not square with our discussion of exclusivity. He had this tryst behind my back. I think back to the night of that date stamp when I got home from work. He claimed that he had been hassled while job hunting, was cross that he had gotten delayed, and supper was not ready when I got home. I suddenly remember that he had tried to pick a fight with me, but I had not been in a fighting mood, and had dismissed it in my mind as a tough day for him. Instead he had had that tryst and was not in any shape for additional sex with me! It makes me furious to realize how he is manipulating me.

I don't know what to do. I rented out my apartment just two months previously and don't feel I can break the lease. And I don't want to stay there, anyway. That place had been robbed while I was in it! The mere thought of staying there gives me an involuntary shudder. So, I can't retreat to my previous life. But what can I do?

I decide to not reveal what I have discovered that day when he gets home, and just observe his behavior going into the future. Is there a pattern to his sudden bouts of bad temper? Could they all be a disguise to cover up a day when he has been out with some other woman? Was that the real reason why he did not want to make love to me that night?

I am glad I have an appointment scheduled with my therapist for the next week. I need somebody whose moral compass might be more trustworthy than my own. Was it right to go into his private desk when my dream warned me to? What about his behavior, when he is not being faithful to me? How can I talk with him about these things when I know some information that I have not gotten legitimately?

I realize that he also has an answering machine that he never checks in my presence. He has set it to pick up messages without broadcasting the speaker's voice, so I cannot inadvertently hear who is calling. If he was not expecting calls from other women, would he have set it up that way?

As it turns out, he never changes his pattern. Although he will never admit it, I am certain he was molested as a child. He does allude to some uneasy times he had as a child, but he also is poorly coordinated, and told me he had been mocked and not liked by other kids. He loves my gentleness and optimism, continues to cook wonderful suppers, and we continue to find interesting art exhibits to attend. It's a stand-off.

However, after eight years of this untrustworthy relationship two events happen that shake me awake. The first one occurs in a hotel restaurant where the chef is known for providing four-star dinners. Of course, it is expensive, and it is rare for my partner to suggest that we be so extravagant. So, when he tells me we are going there, I settle in for a real treat.

During the course of the meal, he leaves the table for the men's room, and our waitress comes up to me. She leans over to speak to me and really stuns me when she says: "Are you his wife? I think you should know that he was here yesterday with a different lady."

Holy cats! What would cause her to say such a thing, even assuming it is true? He is always aloof to serving people, and can be outright rude to them even when they are doing their job well. My best guess is that is what had happened to the waitress the day before. He even might have stiffed her tip completely. And his arrogance would have assured him that he had done the right thing, so he wouldn't hesitate to come back.

Fate provided me the same waitress the next night, and she decided that both she and I deserve better than we were receiving from him! Good for her! I needed that wake-up call. I quietly hide a $20.00 bill under my plate before we leave.

About a week later he is still flush with cash from his latest work and suggests we go out to another new restaurant. This time he insists that a friend has told him about the place, but he has never eaten there. This is another restaurant with heavy, starched white linens on the tables and a Maitre d' with much presence. Enough presence, in fact, to remember this guest's name and say how pleased he is to see him again! Would the gentleman like the same accommodations he had the day before? Since my partner had just repeatedly told me that he had not eaten there before, that provides a little mystery as to how the man could have known his name, never mind his preference for a table!

I add this information to my growing internal list of obviously suspicious behavior. By the time we get home I have decided that that was more than enough data and we need to talk about our obviously broken exclusivity clause.

He will have none of it! He immediately gets angry with me, declares his innocence, says I am paranoid, and on and on. I announce that I am serious, and I am going to call some realtors the next day to have our house appraised, so I can sell it, move out, and move on.

At first, he doesn't believe me, but he can't stop my attempts to create a new future for myself. However, the realtors bring really bad news: we had bought this house together at the very height of the realty bubble, but that bubble had burst shortly after our purchase. It is now several years later, but in the current market we would still owe the bank over $20,000.00 more to repay the mortgage than the house would sell for! Twenty thousand dollars! Yikes!

According to the psychologist Carl Rogers, "The facts are friendly!" — because it is only when you know the facts that you know what you can do! It takes me a whole lot of work to figure out what I can possibly do to fix this situation, even with the supposedly friendly facts at hand.

OK, I cannot move out of the house without losing my share of the money I had invested in it. But I can move out of his bedroom. He has two small offices upstairs and another in the basement. I announce that one of those upstairs rooms is about to become my bedroom, my new bed will be delivered next Tuesday, and he had better have his furniture out of it by then. No negotiations: the bed is going to be delivered, and set up, and the room had better be empty or he will be responsible for setting up my new bed for me! He caves.

So, we start a life where we share a house but not a bed. As time plays out, he realizes that I am set on that arrangement. Many confrontations end with a statement from me such as "Oh, my goodness, you're slipping! Here it is, 6:15 A.M. and that is the first rude thing you've said to me today!" He even learns to be civil to me. Because I demand it.

Eventually the housing market recovers enough so that we can sell the house and break even. That's enough blessing for me. We do sell, and go separate ways. He never learns to have a real relationship with me.

An Aloe Plant to Heal Deep Wounds

I am at a five-day intensive workshop on gender reconciliation. Spirit seems to be heavily involved from the get-go: my favorite teacher is one of the leaders, and she specifically invited me to attend. She had also called and asked if I would pick up one of the men who had to fly in from a distance, and drive him from Boston to upper New Hampshire where the workshop is located.

The workshop is structured for people who have had some gender-related issues in their history. My issues are early childhood sexual abuse. As the participants get to know each other I learn that one lovely lady, who looks like she doesn't have a care in the world, was raped at knife-point. Another woman carries the memories of a physically abusive husband. The men in the group are not immune. One man tells of early childhood sexual abuse, another of repeated physical abuse by his father. The next one was abused by his mother. These anguished tales of woe go on and on.

It is four days into the program. For the first days, we had met for our most intimate work as a woman's group and a separate men's group. My women's group learns to share deeply together, and we are told that the men have as well. But it gets tougher today. We are going to "shadow" the other group: they will meet as if we are not there, and continue their talk. But we will be silent listeners sitting just outside their circle. Then the roles will be switched, and they will shadow our group. I have no idea what will come of it but it feels frightening.

The men talk for quite a while, very respectfully, giving each other encouragement and support by saying "Ho." I'm not sure if Ho has an actual meaning, or if it is just a sound that they use to indicate that the person was heard and understood.

The man I drove to the workshop, who I have become somewhat interested in, takes his turn in the circle, and says "I molested my second wife's daughter from the time she was nine until she was twelve."

I am totally appalled! That could be my molester speaking! I want to scream, but we are constrained to silence as observers around the outer circle, so I cannot make a sound or say anything.

"Ho." Comes the response from the other men in the group.

What? He molested a young girl for years, and all they can say is "Ho?" This adds insult to injury in my brain, which is working overtime by now. I am about to explode.

Luckily, it is time for the men's group observation to come to an end, and we all tumble gratefully into the hall. I head for the Women's room in a turmoil. I want to scream and cry, and don't know what to do. I want to find my teacher, but don't know where to look for her, and I'm going to lose it…

And I do. I leave the bathroom, and realize I am in such physical pain that I can barely walk three steps into the hallway. I drop to my knees, hysterical. I have never done that in my life, but there is no other way to handle the pressure.

I'm sobbing, bent over double in pain, leaning against the wall in the hallway. I don't know who is around me or what is happening… and I don't care. I can't care. All I can do is sob out the horrible pain, the fury, the sense of outrage that all the other men did was say "Ho!" when somebody should have strangled that man for ruining a girl's life! For sentencing her to a lifetime of feeling sullied, never feeling good enough, certainly having no basis for creating boundaries for herself, having no basis for trust in authority figures. A lifetime of painful visits to therapist after therapist! And all the other men do is say "Ho!"

My teacher has found me, and her soft voice is right at my ear, talking me through the pain, through the sobbing, through the condemnation. Once the crying slows down, she takes me outside for a walk. She has brought a glass of water and tissues, and lets me talk, and cry some more, and talk.

Eventually, I stop, exhausted. We rest on the lawn for a short while, then she reminds me that there is a group about to meet inside the building, and asks what I want to do. Am I ready to rejoin them? Do I need to go to my room, and be alone? She is willing to let me do that, but strongly recommends joining the group so we can process what happened in the men's group and my reaction to it. I agree to join the group, although I am not sure that I won't have another breakdown when we reconvene. She reassures me that she'll be right beside me. This is the work we have gathered together to do, and I am in a safe place to do it.

I manage to stay seated next to her in the circle while the group walks in. Directly across the circle from me is the man whose confession had triggered me earlier in the day. He looks as miserable as I feel. And that draws me to him. At least he is feeling more than "Ho."

The group leaders try to process what happened, by congratulating us for having taken the step of coming to the workshop, and being willing to disclose the heavy secrets we have carried for so many years. One of the leaders is a musician, and has provided welcome relief for us throughout the workshop by playing his guitar and singing his music when the tension is too high. He starts strumming a tune, with the refrain "Just one step, that's all it takes…" I am looking across the circle at that man. But he seems utterly dejected, and is staring at the floor in front of himself. He won't make eye contact with anyone in the circle.

Something causes me to look up at the window just a little to his right. On the window sill sits a large aloe plant. I can feel that I'm being prompted: aloe is used for healing…it's a healing plant! I'm feeling pulled to the plant… I want to give it to him… but it is such a risk, and I'm still exhausted from everything that happened earlier.

Finally, I can't stand it. I get up, and with the guitarist still playing, walk across the room "Just one step that's all it takes…." I pick up the aloe plant then bring it inside the circle and stand in front of him with it in my hands.

I look down at him, and he finally looks up. I hand him the plant.

I have never seen anybody so stunned in my life. He stumbles to his feet, and takes the plant from me. Then, with tears pouring down his face, to match the tears on mine, he stammers: "Can…can I give you a hug?"

I nod yes. He hands the plant to the person next to him in the circle, and wraps his arms around me. I return his hug then walk back to my seat in the circle. My face is still wet with tears, but it also wears a radiant smile.

The next day is the end of the workshop, and I drive him back down to Boston. We talk quietly during the ride, sharing what it was like to hold our heavy secrets. He asks if I think he should try to contact the daughter. My mind races, thinking of all the different ways she could receive his contact. I say yes, but caution that she may not be in a space to be receptive. Still, it would be better for him to take the risk than to not contact her. (His relationship with her mother had broken up many years since.)

As I drop him off at the airport, I suggest that we each buy an aloe plant to remind ourselves of the workshop, and he agrees. When I tell my dearest friend about this amazing workshop, she paints a small oil portrait of an aloe plant. I love it! I tuck it on my bookshelf where I can see it from my computer, to remind me of the day.

I have no idea about it at the time, but the aloe plant is going to turn up again in my life, much to my surprise!

Meditation While Going into Surgery

I wrote the notes for this while I was still in the hospital, and then wrote out the details as soon as I got home, three days later, so the memory would still be clear. I needn't have worried. The memory is still clear now as I re-read this story, many years later.

After having meditated with my beloved Tom for many years, I could not meditate alone after he died. It was too lonely, and brought me to that place of being unprotected from my grief from having lost him to cancer. But meditation was my refuge, so I was determined to try again, to prepare for surgery.

It is right there when I need it.

I hadn't known for sure that this would be true. Perhaps I should be ashamed to say that I only went into meditation because I have to, because I have no place else I can go.

I am frightened. I am about to have a total hysterectomy for a cancer in my uterus. Although my son drove me to the hospital, and my sisters joined us before I came upstairs for surgery, I feel the existential aloneness that we all block out most of the time in order to live our lives.

That aloneness is what is so frightening.

The surgery in the operating room where I am scheduled runs over time. They are late calling me. The extra 22 minutes are hard. I alternately talk with my family, fondle a talisman of love that I have tucked into my pocket, and pace the waiting room floor.

When they finally do call me upstairs, and I remove my clothes and don the hospital Johnny, I decide that I will meditate as soon as they let me lie down. I had tried to meditate downstairs earlier, but it was hard to let myself relax, knowing I would have to come upstairs soon.

Finally, they lead me to a gurney in the pre-operation staging area. There are twenty or so such gurneys, each with a person waiting his or her call to an operating room. Each gurney has a series of visitors, checking on the status of that patient as they wait their turn.

I get up on my gurney, lay down on my back, and start to count myself down. "In through the nose, out through the mouth," I remind myself. Five, b-r-e-a-t-h-e i-n.

And Four, e-x-h-a-l-e. And...

A small rectangle, a window, opens just below my right ear. It gives a view of brilliant blue sky and clouds. I don't wonder how it could be behind my ear, with my head lying on the gurney, I just keep counting. I do wonder if it is a gift from my beloved Tom, and from the White Light that he had seen, and from prayers of all sorts that are being said for me. I say a thank you.

And T-h-r-e-e and b-r-e-a-t-h-e i-n....

About that time a young woman comes over with her clipboard, and quizzes me about all the things I have already told them about myself. Yes, that is my name and birth date....

(Keep the slow breathing going.)

...and yes, I have those allergies...

(and exhale and T-w-o...)

...and no, there are no false teeth....

She finally finishes and leaves me alone. I take a slow breath, and go deeper. There is that rich peacefulness and warmth. That beautiful White Light. Total Love.

The anesthesiologist comes by, quizzes me about another whole series of things I have also already told them, and starts the IV drip. I give him a piece of my attention, but don't move all of me out of that safe place. He finishes and leaves.

Another breath, and go deeper.

It is still there...total love....I am totally accepted... cushioned... cared for... at rest. Suspended...held...no fear at all. I am completely loved, in spite of all my imperfections!

A young woman comes over and introduces herself by name. She is the assistant anesthesiologist. How am I feeling?

As I close my eyes again, I tell her that I was anxious earlier, but I am meditating now and I am fine. No, I don't want her shot, unless that would mess up the protocol. In fact, I am feeling so calm I wonder aloud if the anesthesiologist gave me something earlier, when he started the IV.

He arrives back at my gurney at that moment and declares: "Not guilty."

"OK. But no shot, thanks." I smile, because that means the calm comes from that beautiful spot below my right ear.

Both people leave. I open my eyes and glance at the clock. I am saddened to realize that we are running very late. My family will be concerned, because they will think that my surgery or recovery is running long, not that we had started late. And they will not know how peaceful I am. I send them some of the beautiful White Light.

Back to my place of calm and peace. Breathe it in...float...allow myself to feel the love... allow myself to be held, warmed, kept in this beautiful place of safety.

When a nurse comes to wheel me down the corridor, I am glad that we are finally going to get it done, but remain in that lovely, calming space I have found and in touch with my immediate surroundings. I never stop to wonder how I can do that.

The gurney has a square wheel. I joke lightly with the woman who is pushing, then pulling, then wrestling it around corners and through doors...clearly all the men have left now that it is time to do some heavy work.

She pushes the gurney next to the operating table, and asks me to transfer. As I do so, she introduces me to the six people in blue masks and hair nets who are hovering around the operating table. I shift my gaze to take in each pair of eyes between the masks and hair nets, then I giggle and say I hope there will not be a quiz later...they all look exactly the same. They laugh back with me, and I settle in on my new surface.

Another breath, and go deeper. I close my eyes and let the feeling of peace be foremost again. The brilliant blue sky, the gorgeous White Light, the calm. Knowing I am being held. The warmth. The unconditional love.

From time to time for the next little while, I hear them tell me why they are strapping down first one arm, then the next...but I don't let it interrupt my calm.

That is happening out there. The existential me is safe, and somewhere else. That place is lovelier than anywhere else I have ever known. The existential me has found Home.

I don't remember them asking me to count down. The next thing I do remember is my hospital room, the joy of seeing my sons' faces, and an enormous bouquet of flowers from a friend.

Postscript

The operation is a complete success in medical terms. The doctors are thrilled with the way I went through the surgery and recovery. That night the nurses on duty keep trying to teach me how to use the self-administered pain medication attached to my IV, which I haven't touched. I have a hard time convincing them I simply don't need it. I am discharged from the hospital in three days.

Back in my study, I wonder about that place with the feel of Home. And marvel that I was able to go there and be nourished by that beautiful White Light. Then I pick up my book on meditation to continue my reading and my journey.

The Stress of the Dailies

I am panicked. Massachusetts is in a recession, and the company where I had been head of the department has closed its doors. I am trying to be a free-lance tech writer to survive. I accept any job I can find, hoping to land one that will turn into a full-time job with health insurance and other benefits.

It is during this period that I am diagnosed with cancer. I know what cancer means: I will probably not survive very long. I had watched Tom die of cancer in two months, when he was in his 30's!

When I get the diagnoses, I still have medical coverage from my last full-time job and my free-lance boss is willing to let me work from home while I recover from the surgery. So I keep working. I have no choice.

The Social Worker at the hospital tells me not to reveal anything at work about the cancer because I would not be hired full time if they knew. So I don't tell them what the surgery is for.

In addition to paying the bills, work is therapeutic, and I really appreciate that. But my body still needs time to recover from major abdominal surgery, and it is two weeks before I can drive again. Once I do drive, it requires every ounce of energy just to get to work and make it through the day.

Slowly I regain my strength and with it my optimism: they had not found Tom's cancer in time… maybe that will not be true for me. The depth of calm from the experience I had going into surgery holds me in a place of peacefulness. I am not afraid of what death brings. I know it will bring a return to that Peace, that beautiful Light, that Love, to Tom, and to Home.

But as peaceful as I am about death, I also know what dying is like, and it is ghastly. The thought of dying is with me, daily.

And the dailies are hard to take. The job I have is on the far side of Boston from my apartment, which means driving through the city and back out the other side twice a day. I arrange my commute so it is before the rush hour on both ends of the day, but even so I often suddenly find myself in

71

stopped traffic. One day just as I come to a panic stop to avoid a sudden pile-up on the highway, the radio announces that it is 5:43 AM. So, there I am: totally stopped, waiting for the traffic to unsnarl itself, and it is not yet 6:00 in the morning! So much for an earlier commute solving the problem!

That job does not evolve into a permanent position. Nobody is hiring full time, nobody is giving out jobs with insurance benefits, and I am still facing months of follow-up treatments for the cancer. After the last job ends it takes six weeks to find the next job. The work looks promising, but it means driving over 100 miles a day! So, I take that long drive, twice daily. That is a lot of time to spend in the car alone, thinking, worrying about finances.

And worry is what I do. I might not be afraid of death, but I sure am afraid of being broke. Of dying from cancer with no job, no partner, no way to pay for medical treatments! The bills each month are bigger than my part-timer's income, and in between each free-lance job there is a month or two of frantic searching before I can find the next job. A month or two while bills pile up faster. This is one of the hardest periods of my life: I am alone. I am still recovering from the cancer surgery and the after-effects of 31 radiation treatments. I do not have vacation time or sick leave. The period of extended medical insurance from my last real job is running out, and I cannot afford to pay for independent coverage on my erratic income.

One night, after a particularly frustrating day at work, I burst into tears on the long ride home. In anguish about finances, worried about a recurrence of the cancer, about not being able to care for myself in my final illness, about losing my apartment, I cry out "How am I supposed to do this? How can I make it work? I am doing all I can, but I am going to go bankrupt!"

Immediately I hear "You don't have to worry about that."

It is that voice again. That same gentle woman's voice I heard call my name while I was meditating, so many years before. And it fills me with calm. My anxious, hungry soul drinks in that voice, holds it in my heart, takes in its love and welcome message.

By the time I arrive at home I deeply need to absorb the experience and hold it in my heart. So, I undress, wash up, and without bothering with supper go straight to bed. I sleep through the night, almost twelve hours, for the first time in over a year.

The calm of that voice stays with me. Holding me in peacefulness. "I do not need to worry about that." What a blessing.

A few months later, still making that long commute, the thought arises that I might not need to worry about financing a long future because maybe I am not going to live that long! But with that thought comes a smile of peacefulness. I am not worried about death. I was worried about living in an untenable set of life circumstances. But I don't need to worry about that.

A Vision Warns of Betrayal

Eventually I am able to find a real full-time job. Well, make that more than a full-time job! Seventy-hour work weeks are common as this little start-up computer company tries to become viable in the long term. Lots of us new hires were unemployed for a spell before we got these jobs, so we don't bitch about long hours!

It is a busy day and I am at work. I am fully engaged in writing my technical manual, and concentrating hard at my workstation. Something gets my attention in the cubicle next to me, where my boss sits.

I push my rolling chair back to see if he had called to me, or needed me for something. When I am all the way back from my desk, I can see him sitting at a table in the middle of the space between his cubicle and the cubicle across from him. He is laughing and smiling, and talking with the guy next door.

But he has my father's face.

I open my eyes wide, and look again.

Daddy?

I take off my glasses, and rub my eyes, checking whether I have my bifocals on or my reading glasses, which would blur him at that distance. It is the bifocals. I put them back on.

It is definitely Daddy's face!

What is Daddy's face doing on my boss? Daddy, who with his Finnish blood, does not in any way resemble Harry, who looks Mexican. Not Finnish.

Harry is busy, so I can stare at him without attracting his attention. I go inside: "What does Daddy's face mean?"

"Betrayal!"

Whoa! That was instantaneous, and clear! "Why betrayal?"

For all that the first response was instantaneous, there is absolute silence this time. But I'm badly shaken, and a whole lot curious. Why Daddy's face? Why betrayal?

Several times later in the day I check Harry's face at a distance. The superimposed image of Daddy has disappeared. In a way, that's a relief. In another way, it is still puzzling.

That night I meditate on betrayal, and the thought process leads me to my little girl's perception of Daddy leaving me, when he divorced my mother. But how is Harry involved in betraying me?

Within days I get the answer: the economy is threatening to tank again, and since I have a high salary, I'm one of the first on the list to go. So, this vision was a warning about a pending betrayal.

Thank you, Angels! I don't like betrayal, but it does help to be warned that I'm considered dispensable and I better be on my toes!

The Talons—Ready to Strike!

I close my eyes to drop into a guided meditation. The soft voice of my therapist prompts me to move my hand over my heart to feel its beating. It is a fast pulse, and the gesture immediately invokes an image.

There are huge yellow claws—a raptor's talons—poised to snatch my heart. There is almost nothing separating them from my heart but the thinnest layer of… I pause for words to describe it, but I can't. Other parts of the vision are so compelling that I want to take them all in at once.

I can see the raptor's yellow, scaly talons—they occupy the space off to the left of my field of vision. And my heart is exposed to the outside and the talons. From my heart's point of view, I see a field, a sandy road, soft hills one beyond the others, each with fields that lead to other fields. They are planted in rows of lovely growing things, and there is a stream and trees.

Ah! It is the lovely planet, Gaia. My heart is open to it. And the faint separation between my heart and the world is the veil of life. That fragile, slender separation between my soul and the world "out there." I can see how fine, how fragile, it is.

My heart was at risk from the raptor's claws. The separation is thin because my heart is so open to the world. The separation is also thin because our beings are so very fragile. The raptor can see that and is ready to attack this vulnerable one, this wounded one.

"What are the talons?" Asks the voice of my therapist.

The answer comes immediately: "The job I just left! There was so much pressure, so much hate, and I was at real risk while I worked there." I can still see the talons, but they are quiet and closed now, not grasping for my heart.

I hold my hand still, cradling my heart and protecting that gossamer veil. I let the image fade.

R-E-S-P-E-C-T

A different job, a different tough assignment. I am on my way to the office after having told my boss on the phone that a coworker is not being responsive to my role as Team Lead, and I will have to resign. He resents my being Team Lead, and refuses to cooperate with me. You cannot force somebody to do a good job at something if they don't want to do it.

I can no longer give my word that the project will get done on time, properly, completely, or in a way that our very fussy client will approve. After this coworker has made two end-runs around me, and embarrassed the rest of the team with some sexist remarks, I am giving up. But I am worried about the upcoming meeting in which I will bring all this to a head.

Driving to the office, I try to flip to my favorite classical music station, but something makes me go back to the soft rock station —twice!

I'm not particularly listening to the music… when suddenly it grabs my attention: It is Aretha Franklin belting out in her best style: "R-E-S-P-E-C-T, sock it to me, sock it to me … that's all I want is a little RESPECT."

I burst out laughing, and relax. I love synchronicity! Of course, that song is a gift from my deceased partner, Tom. It is a song we often danced to, and it totally matches his sense of humor for the work context that I'm about to face! So, I thank him, and continue on my way.

The next song makes me say out loud: "But this is from Bob!" It is the "I've Got the Leaving You Blues" song that Bob put on his record player when I broke up with him to be in relationship with Tom. Bob had also died a couple years previously.

"So, you two are teaming up and providing my synchronicity musical hits? Neat! And thank you," I say out loud. By this point I am completely relaxed, and feeling that my guardian angels are very close at hand, indeed.

I finish the meeting with my boss, and am driving home… very busy in my thoughts, and concerned about the fallout for my coworker from that meeting. When my boss saw the puny amount of work he had done, she understood what I had been struggling with, and announced that he was going to be fired pronto, and replaced with somebody who would do the job! I would still be Team Lead.

But driving home I am feeling sorry for a fellow human being who is about to lose his livelihood. He was a pain to work with, but I feel some guilt about getting him fired.

What comes on the radio at the next stop light? Quarterflash: "I'm going to harden my heart, I'm going to swallow my tears, I'm going to walk away from you-ou-ou-ou-ou-ou."

Ah, yes! Background music, courtesy of my friends, the Sound Engineers from the Great Broadcast Network in the Sky. Thanks, guys! I giggle all the way home realizing that getting or losing a job is pretty low on the soul's importance scale.

At the Edge of the Abyss

"I am very near the edge."

I am in my usual meditative state in a therapy session, and only realize that I spoke out loud about what I am seeing when my therapist responds.

"What edge? I can think of several you could be approaching."

I have just actually seen The Edge. It looks like the literal edge of a cliff, with a sheer, bottomless, drop-off on the side. But it's obviously a symbolic Abyss, and the way it glows with internal light marks it as a clear archetypical vision.

I am pretty terrified of heights. I hate buildings with glass walls overlooking a multi-story atrium. I cannot go near the glass without feeling dizzy.

But this Edge is different. It is just there. I think my comment is one of wonder and surprise that I can be so near it, right at an unprotected drop off, without my usual fear.

I can see the drop-off.

I know I could fall.

But I am only observing it. For that split-second in eternity, I am not afraid of heights.

In fact, I know I am not afraid of death; perhaps the vision is only reinforcing that knowledge.

This vision precedes a session of intensely deep work, some of which is acutely painful, as I reluctantly face my demons. The session requires processing over a number of days. I am used to that by now.

I am near an abyss: a bottomless pit of despair, rage, and hopelessness that threatens to overwhelm me at times. But as has happened several times before, it does resolve. I know it is over when I can meditate again. And my meditation brings me back to a point where I can think of everyone in my life with compassion and love.

Aloe Plant, the Next Generation

I am sitting at my computer proof-reading an email I am about to send to a former friend and business partner. We have come to some severe disagreements in which I feel he is being unprofessional and perhaps shady in his dealings with others. I feel betrayed and outraged, but I am trying to keep those feelings in check. The email spells out how we will sever our relationship in great detail.

I have been working on the email, and my internal states, for almost 12 hours. I have recently read Emotional Genius by Karla McLaren, and the book is very clear about what I should and should not do when I am furious. No matter what, I must remain civil and fair.

I think I have finally worked out the email and the conditions for separating in a way that requires the same amount of work from both of us. But I am leaving a door open to meet one last time to discuss the situation.

So, I am sitting at my computer, proofreading previously written text, not even typing on the keyboard, except to take out an occasional comma. I hear a sound slightly to my right, but mostly in front of me… it is coming from the bookcase, which I can just barely see out of my peripheral vision. I notice a fast movement… something has just fallen off the bookcase.

I look beneath my computer table, and right there, facing me, under the email I am proofing, is the oil painting a friend made for me of the aloe plant. I have kept the painting on that bookcase to remind myself of the day when a real aloe plant played such a huge role of healing and reconciliation in my life.

The picture cart-wheeled off the bookshelf, and landed upside-down on its top edge. Further, it ricocheted off of something in order to stop a good three feet to the left of where it would have been, if it had just fallen straight down. And it ended up facing me! Alternatives:

- It could have stayed put! Nothing else in the room chose to jump off the bookshelf at that point… it is not like we had an earthquake or something!

- It could have fallen straight down, in which case I would have had a hard time reaching it because there is furniture in the way. I might not have seen it, or I might have ignored it until my (almost finished) task was complete and I had sent the email.

- It could have fallen in such a way that it was not facing me.

- It could have fallen when I was not even in the room, and didn't know about it!

- It seems pretty obvious that it must be a blessing from one of my more active angels!

Ok, who's acting up? What spirit is trying to get my attention? You were gloriously successful, of course!

The aloe plant picture is standing on its head, and it looks so foolish that I have been convulsed with laughter. I stop laughing to try to catch my breath, only to start up again. And your next act, my energetic spirit-friend?

I quickly find out what that next act is. After I laugh for five minutes, I go to call my sister to tell her, as she is one of the few people who knows what the aloe picture stands for. First, I cannot find the card with her office number on it in my Rolodex. When I finally find it, I take it out to see her office number on the back of the card, and the card spirals out of my fingers, and drops out of reach under my desk. Guess this is a day when things are spiraling all around my office! Alrighty, then! I'm not supposed to call her.

I got what I am supposed to not do. But I am supposed to do what??? Well, nobody seems to be stopping me writing this Journal page...so far at least! Guess that is a thing I am allowed to do!

After recording all of those shenanigans in my Journal, I return to my email task. I radically revise the text so it is much gentler, more open-ended, and is worlds away from the last version. Hopefully this version will not cause anything else to jump off the bookcase.

Well, not the bookcase... but my email stops working. Then my whole computer crashes! I give up! I go for a long walk, and just hand the situation over to whomever feels more in control of this issue than I do! And I laugh every few minutes, for the silliness of it all.

The next day I discover that I have lost the unfinished email and have to start anew. But it is just as well. The next day also brings a calmer approach to the situation. I write the email quickly, print it out and re-read it (just to be sure), and send it on its way. Deed done, with grace and no rancor, thanks to an aloe plant standing on its head. And the spirit who put it there!

A Near-Miss on a Drive to the Airport

We are living in a suburb some 20 miles south of Boston, almost into Rhode Island. I work on the famous Route 128 belt around Boston, so my commute is pretty tough just to get home in the evening. This afternoon, once I get home, I am going to have to drive back into the city again. My partner has to catch an international flight out of Boston's airport on a Friday evening in the summer. Lousy timing! Route 128, the circumferential highway, could be stopped altogether!

It is the same around most cities: Friday night's commute is particularly tough, with people trying to get away for the weekend. So, I am concerned about the drive back into the city, and getting to the airport on time. A major slow-down or an accident could make my partner miss his plane. So, I take the whole afternoon off from work to make a trip that should take one hour!

We load his suitcases into the car, and out of habit I ask my angels for a safe trip, and that we get there on time. The first leg of the trip is totally straight-forward and we have no problems. On the next leg, I know the spots where merging traffic creates potential slow-downs. Just as we approach the first one, I can see the cars ahead of me start to slam on their breaks. As I hit my breaks, I scream "No, angels, No!"

Immediately I am 12 feet above my car, observing the accident about five cars ahead of me. I see a green sedan, which has been side-swiped, limping off the road to the right break-down lane. The cars around him, all of which had stopped, are cautiously beginning to inch forward. Another badly dented car, a blue hatch-back, also makes it to the shoulder. More cars start to move again.

Snap! I am suddenly back behind the steering wheel of my car again. Only seconds have passed, if that. I am more than a little shaken, but my car was never in danger. The road has now opened up again, and traffic is moving.

The rest of the trip slips by without incident and we make it to the airport with time to spare. I offload my passenger and get back on the highway.

But I have a lot to think about on my way back home. And ever since: How did I get out of the car and observe the accident from above? Who was driving the car while I was up there? How did my car stay "under control?" Who was in control? If that was what is called an "out-of-body experience," what was my body doing while I left?

I have read about people being out of their body under hypnosis, while meditating, while asleep, and during near-death experiences. I have never read about somebody having one while driving in heavy traffic. Don't try this at home, kids; I lived through it, but I do not recommend it.

Going Home

When Tom and I used to sail on his boat off Marblehead, he would play various pieces of classical music on the very good sound system he had installed on board. One of our favorites was the Fifth Symphony by Dvorak. In particular, the "Going Home" theme from that work. Tom would wrap his long arms around me and snuggle while that theme was playing. Once, early in our relationship, he had whispered into my ear "You are my home," as we sailed, and listened to the music, and watched the beautiful play of sunlight on water.

That piece of music hovers around me. At the small franchise restaurant when Tom's family and I are planning Tom's funeral, it suddenly is on the sound system. I am so stunned to hear it, I virtually shout: "Listen!"

As those around the table stop their conversation, I tell them that it was one of Tom's favorite selections, and it is promptly added to the music for his memorial service.

Then, more than three decades later, I am estranged from my partner of the last ten years, and we have sold the house that we had bought together. I have finally packed the last of my belongings, and I get into my car to drive away. As I start the motor, the radio automatically comes on. Sailing loud and clear across the air waves: the theme from Going Home. I break into tears of joy. Indeed, I am going to a new home and a new life!

Synchronicity, I love it! It has provided a musical background to my life that would rival the best movie director's choices.

When I think about the afterlife, the phrase that comes to mind has always been "going Home." Others have written about it in this same way… it is a journey to my spirit's Home. I am not worried in the slightest about what it is like there. Getting there might be a problem, and I worry sometimes about a protracted, painful death. But other than the pain of leaving my family and loved ones behind, I am not afraid of dying. I will just be finally going to my real Home. And I will be with Tom.

My Lunch Buddy at Work

We are sitting at our usual place in the noisy cafeteria. One reason we meet for lunch is because we have similar home libraries—books about meditation, the afterlife, mysticism, reincarnation. Not the kind of things you talk about with everyone at work. But trustworthy indicators that this particular person at work will have lovely insights into things I care about.

However, we have both been rather silent at lunch lately. I'm fighting depression again. I assume my friend has been quiet because of fatigue from the chaos of work.

Our lunch date today turns out to be unusual.

My friend tells me about talking with his mother about how our souls persist from life to life. He is trying to convince her how living continues on the other side, how we remain connected to those we have loved and lost, and how we reincarnate over and over.

He is talking very gently as he relates how he slips one little concept after another to her in a way she can take in. How she is very skeptical, but he eases this knowledge in to her so she can assimilate it. In a total role reversal, he is the teacher and his mother is the pupil.

As he is telling me this, his face changes completely. His eyes soften and light up with a wonderful glow as the tension in his face dissolves so that it is soft and open.

Watching him as he tells me all this, first I see a wispiness, then I see a different face in front of his face. I am watching him transform in front of my eyes.

He talks on for quite a while as I watch him, transfixed.

When he stops, I tell him: "I wish you could see your face as you are talking about this! I think I am seeing your Spirit! This must be your life work… the work your soul has come to Earth to do… to help your mother in this way. You are entranced when you talk about this!"

He smiles gently, but that visual shift I had seen dissipates as he looks at me. The lines of tension return, and his normal wary self is back.

He is curious about what I said, and asks me to repeat it. As I do, he nods in agreement. "Do you think so? Yeah, that feels right," he says thoughtfully.

Both feel right. It is his life work, or at least part of it. And I have seen his Spirit.

I have seen this blurring of a face and the appearance of the Spirit before. The first time was shortly before Tom was hospitalized with his final illness. A cloudy substance appeared in front of his eyes, then the shape of his face changed. It was unsettling, but not particularly frightening. I didn't know what to make of it. I still don't know if it foretold his death.

The next time a person's face blurred on me was when I was talking with my sister, who had just been through a traumatic incident when one of her children had been hospitalized. She was relating the events to me, and was reliving them in all their intensity. I was concerned about her welfare, and how she could recover from so much emotional pain. I cautioned her to be very careful in everything she did. She was in a very vulnerable place and I didn't want her to have an accident.

I still don't know why I have been able to see these things, but the feeling from the events is clear: I am privileged to sometimes see Spirit. It is very humbling.

Whisper, No Words

Somebody whispered to me yesterday as I was walking down the street.

I never walk along that sidewalk, as it abuts a busy highway with strip mall stores and small parking lots, lots of exhaust smell, and not much pleasant to see.

I have gone into one shop, and I know I want to visit another shop a short block away. I decide to park once, and walk to the other shop from where I am parked. It is a lovely spring day and I can use some exercise in the sun.

My first stop is at a framing store. I am kept waiting for over 20 minutes for a simple transaction, and am then scolded by the counter person for fitting my photograph into the frame I am buying before I pay for it. I react with a curt statement about how I have injured nothing, I already have the cash out on the counter to purchase the item, and I have been kept waiting for an inordinate amount of time.

Walking to the next store in a huff, I hear a whisper in my left ear. No words, but a distinct whisper, and the feel of the breath, so I wheel around to see who is so close to me when I am walking so fast. There can't be anyone there; it is not physically possible....

And, of course, there is no one.

I stop in my tracks, and quickly go within to try to figure out what I had heard and felt. It was a whisper. Nothing sounds quite the same as a whisper. There had been a lull in the traffic, so there were no trucks going by with their air hoses, nothing that would have made a whooshing sound. No moving cars in a nearby parking lot. There is no breeze at all. There is nothing and nobody near me. But I have just heard a whisper. With no words. And I feel a presence beside me that cannot be denied!

I realize that I have just been chided for my behavior. Yes, I could have been a lot more patient with that store clerk. I feel contrite, and I will try to do better.

Peeling a Purple Onion

I am lying on Lisa's Polarity Therapy table, and we are doing intense work on my belly. I'm feeling my uterus and ovaries, despite the fact that they were surgically removed over ten years ago.

I have the sense of Here we Go Again! One more time, working on the childhood abuse and the petty abusers who followed later, working on my sexuality, the losses that surround my sexuality, including cancer of the uterus.

Hoping against hope, I think maybe if I go to the bathroom, it will just turn out to be a full bladder. Mission accomplished, the feelings are still there: it is the uterus. And the feelings are so strong they are nearly like the menstrual cramps I have not had for years. I hate it! Aargh! But I am here to do the work that presents itself, and this must be the work for today.

We work for a while in silence. She concentrates on my torso, gently touching one place and then another; I lie there, meditating with my eyes closed, maintaining a receptive state to encourage healing. Then I get a stunning image of an enormous red onion. Layer after layer of white onion flesh, with the thin red coat… blood red…bleeding uterus, bleeding cancer, red….

I see the onion's layers break away one by one as Lisa tells me to breathe in through a particular spot in my belly. The chunks of layered onion lay all around the central piece we started with, bathed in brilliant white light.

Finally, a shift in my energy! I feel it clearly: it is a real release from the tightness and muddy pressure I had been experiencing before. Lisa says triumphantly "There it is!" and moves to a different place on my body.

She's right about my body, but my mind stays with my onion. And my mind is finding it funny.

Lisa checks in with her quiet voice: "Where are you? What are you feeling now?"

I don't want to focus on feelings, I'm finding my mental picture so exquisitely complete it could pose for a still life photo. All these chunks of beautiful onion, tinged with red…

But it is also funny, so I say "I don't know what I'm feeling. My mind is caught in a vision and a thought: Do you know what you get when you break down an onion, layer by layer, by layer?"

Lisa asks for the answer.

"Onion!"

She howls with laughter, as do I!

And all the pent-up energy of the work we've just done dissolves out of my body as we laugh together for a full minute or two. I'm so relieved and delighted that this quirky, funny visual image I was given in such exquisite detail is also funny to her! I am stunned by the fact that we can communicate so perfectly in our second session together.

After we can breathe again, I describe the image to her, and stress that it was a red onion... then I realize: Oh, of course! I'm wearing a cranberry red turtleneck today to be matched perfectly by my blood-red onion!

Tuning In, Tuning Up

I am walking along a tree-lined street in a suburb of Boston. I have driven here to take a class and I have a half hour to spend walking. I arrive early so I can let go of the alertness I need to drive, and start to enter the calm, centered state I need to meditate. It is a lovely summer evening, and I breathe it in, lower my gaze, and start a walking meditation.

As I slowly pace along the sidewalk, I feel a sensation of being pulled gently upward, as if the energy in my brain is being magnetically attracted to something high above me. At the same time, I sense a sweetness... I do not really taste it, but sense it. I pause to investigate what is happening. I feel like I have expanded upward and outward.

I look up, and into the canopy of leaves of a huge old Sugar Maple tree. Oh, that's it! I am sensing the sweetness of the maple, and my energy has been swept upward to join the energy field of that huge old tree. Is it that same force that pulls moisture up from the tree's roots all the way to its topmost leaves, that has pulled me along with it? I stand looking up into the leaves for a couple minutes, smiling, rejoicing in the sensation of the tree's energy. Savoring that subtle flavor from its sweet sap. Maple syrup, indeed.

I resume my stroll, feeling centered and at peace with this lovely planet, grateful for the beauty everywhere. I am about to pass under the next tree. I close my eyes and with a sense of curiosity just allow myself to feel. Yes, it feels different. I am now in the energy field of a large cedar tree, and the sweetness of the maple has been replaced with a slightly acrid sensation. It is not a taste, but it is an awareness in my mouth, nose, and sinuses. I look up into its canopy of needles, and wonder at this process. Grateful for the beauty of this big old tree. Loving it, but keenly aware that it is not as sweet a sensation as the maple!

Once again, I resume my walk, passing alongside a vibrant six-foot tall hedge of tiny brilliant green leaves. Suddenly I feel a frightened reaction, and look over to see what the hedge is sharing with me. Frightened? It has thousands upon thousands of tiny oval leaves arranged on short branches. It is huge, vibrant green…what does it have to be frightened of?

Gently, I reach for a sprig of its leaves, and suddenly feel the bristle of an undercoating made up of as many thorns beneath the stem as there are leaves on the top of it. The thorns are not visible when I look at it; but they are there to protect the delicate, succulent leaves from browsers.

Browsers? There have been no sheep or goats to eat this bush in this neighborhood in a couple hundred years! But it remains true to type, protecting itself against such a possible attack. The thought comes: am I protecting myself against something equally as unlikely? Do I have a bristly underside as a protective device, whether I need it or not? Is that the message from this tall and stately hedge?

It is time for class, so my question goes unanswered as I hasten my steps. I feel alert and fully alive. Privileged to be on the planet, to be able to sense it in so many ways. I am still such a novice in meditation! There is so very much to learn, to sense, to understand.

I suddenly remember the beauty of the energy field around a single maple leaf that I had seen in a book of Kirlian photographs. Imagine what a whole tree's energy field must look like, if you could but see it! I didn't see it, but moments ago I felt it, and it is glorious!

I marvel at the many different energies around me. Then I remember a story from my reading: the Buddha sat under a tree to meditate and found enlightenment. Indeed!

Gift of a Vision

I'm lying on Pamela's therapy table, as she plays her music for me. I ask for something peaceful, as I have been fighting demons for weeks and have been in a state of deep depression. I'm crying as I relate the depths that the last weeks have held for me. Her quiet, nurturing voice bids me to allow my body to relax onto the table now and let go of whatever I am carrying. She guides me into a deep state of meditation.

The music comes on, and it is a day when I can see colors — something that looks like the aurora borealis— waves of color that shimmer and move in time to the music. It is always strikingly beautiful: evanescent and deeply moving. Sometimes there are showers of colors, sometimes lines or dots of color. Other times it is a shimmer like the lovely surface of a bubble. I don't always see it. It is a real treat when I do.

With the music, fleeting sensations come. First, I see light dancing off water. Then I feel like I'm being held. I don't know by whom, but it feels wonderful and familiar. It feels like Tom when we were sailing on his boat. Certainly, my soul is being held as I sink deeper into the Alpha state. Pamela changes the music. Suddenly I am being shown a vision.

I see a woman standing alone, surrounded by swirling, glistening light. I'm drawn to her familiarity… Am I seeing myself? Then I think, No! She is young; she can't be me! She is so lithe and effortlessly erect. Immediately the answer comes back: "Not young, ageless; yes, I am you."

As I look at her, I remember the vision I had of Tom after he died. I saw his soul, his total essence: whole and perfect. It was not just that he was OK, or well again (after the devastation of the cancer), he was whole, filled with joy, and he was perfect.

This is the same vision of a soul, except that this time it is my soul. I am there, joyfully standing in the light and perfect. I can hardly breathe, it is so lovely. It had never occurred to me that I could see my own soul.

I certainly have never thought of myself as perfect! This personality called "Rosey" acts out so often, how could I think of myself that way? But here is a Rosey who is perfect.

Now, in awe, I absorb the deep meaning of love and peace that she presents to me in striking clarity.

Earlier in the session I had said that I want to relate to people on a soul level. With slightly arched eyebrows, Pamela quietly suggested that I have pretty high standards! Well, I guess so. But if this is seeing on a soul level, it is a glorious gift!

How do I know it's a vision? Maybe I'm making it up for myself? Riding home, I think about the vision… I used to be a costume designer, so if I had set myself the task of drawing my soul, I would have presented it so that it filled my field of vision. This vision is off to my left side, and at a distance. The remainder of my field of vision is blackness… but with a shimmer of red to it, a liveliness, not a flat black.

And my soul is surrounded by swirling light in my vision. She is wearing a long, form-fitting white gown that gleams, almost as if it is its own source of light. In a meditative vision, it is always clear where the objects are in space relative to where I am in that same space… and they are never where I expect to find them. It is somebody else's intelligence that has created this vision for me. And it is far lovelier than I could have created it.

That was yesterday, in Pamela's therapy room. As I sit here now, typing with my eyes closed, the vision returns, then slightly turns to face me. As she does so, she changes. Today, it is not just my soul I am seeing, I am seeing the universal soul… it is not just my soul that is perfect… all souls are perfect. Absolutely free, whole, filled with joy, and perfect. Is this the mystery of religions that assert that there is no wrong or right? That all actions are just different ways to express our free will?

I stop typing, and walk around my apartment, deeply engrossed in thought. On one hand, I feel that it is truly wrong to hurt somebody else. But on the deepest level, we cannot hurt anyone else's soul. Even in the worst case, all they do is to return Home.

Possibly somebody can damage his or her own soul, but this message that has been presented to me says that nobody can damage another soul. Damage a personality, and a person, of course! But the soul remains perfect, safe from harm.

It would be good for me to try to remember this the next time I feel awash in anguish, because somebody denigrates me! My personality may feel deep loss, grief, or anger but my soul remains perfect, unsullied, whole, and radiant with joy. What I thought was a soul-level wound was not so. The soul cannot be wounded. It remains upright, lithe, lovely, and joyful.

Meditations on a Vision of my Soul

I have been given an enormous gift: I have been allowed to see my soul. I am astonished. I had seen my beloved Tom's soul after he died, but that was his generous gift to me. Seeing his soul helped alleviate my devastating grief. Today, from the blackness of despair, I see my own soul.

I am stunned by her beauty. *She is perfect!*

I thought my soul had been horribly disfigured by the childhood sexual abuse. *It wasn't!*

I thought my soul was marred by the rejection I felt from the divorce. *Not a blemish!*

I thought my soul had transgressed horribly, when meditating for healing failed to "cure" Tom, and he died of cancer as a very young man. I thought that transgression was on the soul level. *I did not transgress, it was not on the soul level, or both.*

Watching Tom die was traumatizing. *The trauma did not harm my soul.*

I have spent much of my adulthood in deep depression, self-loathing, and physical pain. *My soul is pain-free and filled with joy.*

I have felt intense fury when I have been falsely accused. *My soul is not angry and feels no righteous indignation.*

Without even needing to use words, my soul conveys to me that all souls are perfect. I am part of All Souls, and *all souls are perfect. My molester's soul, my accuser's soul, all souls.*

I stand erect in the Light, and in my perfection, as does every other soul. The Light shines through the eternal blackness of ignorance to provide this stunning display.

How I Found Swedenborg Chapel

I have been seeing Pamela, my therapist, pretty regularly, trying to make sense of the huge transition I am making from working life to retirement. The day I tell her about the vision of my soul she comments, "Rosey, you are such a mystic, have you tried Swedenborg Chapel?"

Surprised to be dubbed a mystic, and surprised more by the suggestion that I become involved with any organized religion, I ask for more information. "Well, they're right here in Cambridge and you might enjoy a community of like-minded souls."

As always, it is offered as just a suggestion, and during the next busy month or so, I completely forget about it. Until one Sunday morning, when I wake up saying out loud, and with considerable emphasis: *"Swedenborg!"*

That gets my full attention! I don't remember a dream, or anything in particular that prompts me to say the name of this mystic, but I go on line to track down this mysterious Swedenborg Chapel.

I browse their web site, www.swedenborgchapel.org, and decide almost instantly to go to church that beautiful sunny morning. As I have plenty of time before church, I click on their link to previous sermons, in order to see a sample of what I will be hearing from the altar. I select a sermon by Rev. Sarah Buteux called "Giving from the Heart." I understand about giving, but I discover to my surprise that the sermon is about tithing, which is giving 10 % of your income. I read on, and find the following statement:

> *"We are a diversely talented and generous group of people. I am so thankful for each and every one of you because you so freely share your computer skills, your artistic ability, your knowledge of home improvement, your ideas for how we can strengthen our efforts, and your compassion for one another. Even taking the time to come to church on Sunday is an act of giving. I hope you know how valuable your presence here this morning is to our community and our future."*

"Even taking the time to come to church on Sunday is an act of giving?" I repeat, somewhat incredulously. I am stunned and ask out loud: "Are you talking to me?" I laugh at this delightful instance of synchronicity, shut down my computer, and go to meet this lovely community of like-minded souls.

I am welcomed with open hearts, and a joyous interest in the new stranger in their midst. The interim pastor captures my full attention. As I keep asking about different aspects of Swedenborg's philosophy, she gives me first one book, then another… finally I get five books for my library! Five books! I've found heaven in Cambridge, Massachusetts! I scurry home and start reading these books that I have received. In them I find wonderful beliefs that help me understand some of my visions.

According to Swedenborg, we cast off our sickly earthly bodies at death, and take the form of our eternal spirit. We get younger in appearance, until we appear as if we are in our thirties. The source of all love and wisdom does exist in Heaven, and it is perceived as radiant light. (This must be the beautiful White Light that Tom saw in his meditation and that I saw during surgery!) We have the opportunity to learn more about the lessons we didn't finish in our earth-bound life; we are continually learning and growing.

We live in communities of like-minded souls with our soul mate. Swedenborg had not been able to connect with his soul mate while alive, but he knew that she would be waiting for him when he returned to his spiritual state. In my case, I will be able to return to my beloved Tom! Just as he said when he visited me after he died!

95

After I have read the introductory books about Swedenborg, I turn to his own writings, and I find some of them to be slow going. Swedenborg knew the theology of his day and what his distracters would say once they saw his writings, so he pre-empted their criticisms up front. It helps to read Swedenborg for the first time in a group of people who already know him.

I need help understanding this amazing theological material. So, I join the Thursday Night Reading Group at the Chapel, and start getting to know this scientist who became a mystic. He had deeply moving experiences; and an amazing life! I have found the answers my restless soul has been seeking these many, many years.

4 Thoughts on Years of Reading

I have probably read hundreds of books on meditation, spirituality, synchronicity, and all their associated subjects. I find that there are repeated themes throughout those books.

Different Sources, Common Ideas

When I start to compile the "Ex Libris" chapter, I have a great time going from one bookcase to another, pulling six or eight books at a time off the shelves and carrying them to the computer so I can capture their titles, authors, and publishers. It is like greeting old friends, some of whom I have not seen for years.

Before long, I have stacks of books on the floor encircling my chair. To refresh my memory, and in order to write the annotations, I open each in turn, and am amazed how quickly the essence of each book comes back to me.

I have now spent portions of several weeks doing this, and am vividly aware of the common threads in these books. Here are some of them.

Ground Yourself in Prayer or Meditation

It doesn't matter what form the prayer takes, but the power that you are invoking in meditation must be accepted with a humble heart. Pray for humility, and that you may be allowed to be a channel for blessings and healing for someone you love.

If you are comfortable praying to God, or other named being from a specific faith, by all means do so. If you are not comfortable with that, ask for help from a higher power, or Spirit, or from the White Light. The White Light has appeared to people of many faiths across the centuries in the recorded histories of many different civilizations. And, undoubtedly, in unrecorded civilizations as well.

Surround Yourself with the White Light

Surround yourself, and those on whom you want to focus your blessings, with the White Light. Some meditative practices incorporate quite a bit of ritual to keep negative thoughts and influences at bay. The White Light knows how to protect you, so I don't believe you need to use elaborate rituals. But do ask for its protection.

Find a Meditation Mentor

Many of the books that teach meditation caution that you should have a mentor to whom you can relate anything. If you sit long enough in meditation you will have strange experiences that you simply cannot explain in any way that fits within the Western-scientific view of "normalcy." My very strange experiences prove that!

During the meditation when I saw an acquaintance sprout devil's horns, it was horribly frightening, and I didn't know what to do about it. It took me many hours of reading and talking with my mentor to calm down.

At that time, I was meditating more than once daily, but I couldn't return to meditation until I was able to come to grips with that experience. First my mentor and I examine the entire content of the meditation in the context of what that person represents in my life. Then we decide that the horns are simply a visual clue that the person was not helpful (therefore, "not good") in the context of the healing I was requesting. The horns did not imply that the person was "the devil incarnate." This man just wanted to do other things, such as astral projection and age-life regression, with time spent in the Alpha state.

So, I came to believe that the message of that vision was that those things were not good for me. The horns were my mind's non-verbal way to say so. After all, what other way could you symbolically indicate that those things were bad for me?

And that visual representation certainly got my attention! I paid heed. Voluntary astral projection has been missing from my intended activities (although it did appear very unexpectedly, once, as you read elsewhere in the book)!

Remember Meditation Etiquette

Be respectful of what you do in meditation. Stay positive. I go into meditation knowing that I have a deep respect, bordering on fear, for the power that can be invoked. Because one book leads to another, and many lead to reincarnation, I wonder if I have been on the meditative path before. I also wonder whether I ever slipped into trying to use meditation for selfish purposes. Or if someone else thought I was doing that, and punished me "appropriately." (As in the Salem witch trials?)

If I do have a past-life remembrance of being punished, it may be justified. I have seen the beauty and power that can be invoked. I have lived the blessing of being connected to another through Spirit. All this is humbling, but it is also mercurial: it makes me want to say, "Wow! Look what I just did!!!" And the exact second that it shifts from my humble awareness of its being a gift to feeling that I am the creator of these blessings, I have to go deep within and give thanks for the gifts. They are not by me, they are through me. And they are sacred.

Be Grateful for Your Blessings

Have a thankful heart. Instead of counting down, occasionally start your meditation by letting your mind drift from one person you love to another, staying with that person just long enough to bless their essence, and then gently moving to another person. Hold a thankful feeling in your heart for the blessings you have received through your contact with each soul.

You can use this spirit of thankfulness to take the bite out of an irritation in your life, whether it is small or large. When I was first learning about healing meditation, I undertook the discipline of giving thanks for irritants in everyday life.

I get irritated in traffic, and twice daily as I commute, I allow myself to fuss and curse and get into a real state of aggravation. So, for my first discipline in giving thanks for irritants, I decide that every time the driver ahead of me is going too slowly, I will immediately express gratitude for that driver instead of allowing myself to get angry.

Sounds crazy? Try it! On my first attempt at this discipline, I get a dose of instant karma that still makes me smile.

For starters, I am habitually late. I am always blustering along the road, driving too fast, and upset that I'll be embarrassed by my own chronic lateness.

One night I am in a hurry to get to my prayer and meditation group, and I am on a two-lane road creeping behind somebody who is driving exactly at the speed limit. Everybody knows you can drive five miles over the limit, right? I am fidgeting behind the wheel and consider breaking the law by passing him. But I suddenly remember that my spirituality exercise is to hold him in my heart and give thanks that he is there.

So, I do so. I firmly tell myself to suspend disbelief, and I say out loud: "Thank you that this person is driving down this road right now, helping me remember to drive safely and not to break the speed limit."

Two hundred yards later we both pass a very well-hidden State Trooper, waiting for those without a thankful heart, who are in too much of a hurry!

Amen, Amen! And thank you, Angels! I giggle all the way to the group, and am still laughing when I relate the results of my weekly discipline.

Stay Upbeat

If you lead anyone else in meditation, be careful what you say; keep your statements positive. You are leading them into an Alpha state, and when people are in Alpha, they are highly susceptible to suggestion. This is very similar to the state of hypnosis. The mind is very literal and, although there is probably a self-protection mechanism at work, you would not want to say something that the mind would react to too literally.

Because of this, I simply ask the White Light to perform its healing. I don't know how bodily processes take place, but the White Light does. So, I just ask for that wisdom to do the work, if there is any un-ease or disease.

Notice Your Meditation's Scope

There are times when my meditations are peaceful, but not particularly memorable. I leave the meditation refreshed, but with no specific thoughts or memories of the event. There are other times, when I have had thoughts and visions that were clearly not created by my mind at all. These gifts of the spirit are profoundly different from anything I could have made up in my own mind.

In these meditations, if I see something, it is bathed in light. Figures gleam with internal light and there is a sense of energy about the whole scene that is exquisitely beautiful.

At other times, whatever I am seeing either does not make sense (such as a window that appears behind my right ear, while I am lying on my back), or it is presented in terms that are different from the way I would have created it. Sometimes I see clues that the vision is other-worldly. For instance, beings are surrounded by beautiful blue sky and wispy white clouds. I may also get a keen feeling of anticipation, as if I know that something wonderful is about to happen. As if someone is whispering in my ear "Pay attention, Rosey! This is especially for you!"

I treasure these times. They lead me to continue meditating, continue my reading, and to try to live a life that is worthy of such gifts. These experiences are gifts from that place of unconditional love called Home.

Find Healing in Meditation

Allow your meditations to heal you. I have had intermittent periods when I can't sleep well. I am either not able to get to sleep or I wake in the middle of the night and cannot get back to sleep. Either form of sleeplessness is a problem when I have to be at work the next day in a job that requires extended periods of concentration. So, when I can't sleep, I meditate to heal my body of its fatigue.

The literature on the Alpha state is very clear: twenty minutes of meditation restores your body as completely as four hours of sleep! So, if I am wakeful in the night, I meditate and hold myself in a calm mental state about the lack of sleep, knowing I have done everything I can to enable myself to get through the next day. And then I do my best to keep my lack of sleep out of my mind during the day.

After all, if you go around telling others that you're tired from lack of sleep, your body hears you, you know! And it will be all too willing to feel appropriately tired when you have told it that it should!

Hold those comments about fatigue until bedtime. Then thank your body for carrying you through the day. At bedtime tell it that now is a fine time to feel fatigue and sleepiness.

Sweet dreams, and lacking that, may your meditations be peaceful and full of meaning.

Meet Your Soul Mate?

So, you just met somebody wonderful, and you think: is this the one? Is he (or she) my soul mate? How can you tell? Your sensations will surely be different from mine, but when I met Tom, I was completely swept off my feet. He felt different from anybody else I'd ever met!

For one thing, the first time he held me, I could feel his energy all around me. Years later, after I'd learned about auras, I realized that I could feel his aura enfold me. I'd never felt anything even close to that! It felt safe and caring, but also vibrant. There was a joyousness about it. It felt like I was opening up a huge gift, unlike any other I'd ever come upon.

I certainly had no idea at the time, but it was an opening to all of my meditative experiences, and that does make it the biggest gift I have ever received. It was like somebody who is destined to become a virtuoso performer receiving their first violin. They may feel excited about receiving the gift, but they cannot know the potential they will reach with it. They cannot know that it will become the most important thing in their life!

And this may be a clue to whether a particular person is really your soul mate: I felt a huge sense of gratitude. An overwhelming sense that I had just been blessed with something far beyond anything I had known before. I was very grateful.

Keep Learning

Take classes, read books, read the blogs of other meditators on line and watch them on TV, find a support group in your area. Check out the Association for Research and Enlightenment (the A.R.E. that was founded by Edgar Cayce) as they have mini bible study groups everywhere and they welcome new members.

You don't necessarily have to agree with everything that is in a book or in the beliefs of a study group. I am not Catholic, but I have found many books by Catholic priests and nuns to be uplifting and enriching. The same is true for books by Buddhists; I do not follow the same spiritual practices, but I find enrichment for my own practice within what they believe.

5 Ex Libris

My sons grumble every time they help me move because of the number of boxes of books! And I can't blame them! There are a lot. And those boxes are heavy. But these are books! They are my inspiration. My solace. My friends.

Welcome to My Library

In the 35-plus years that I've been meditating, I've read books on meditation as a religious practice, books on the Alpha state and how it can be invoked by slowing the mind and breath, books on meditating for healing, and treatises on the physics of the time-space continuum, and how mind, thought, and spirit are all part of that gestalt.

While I was brought up Christian, and there are Christian books listed here, I don't believe that Christianity (or any other religion) has a lock on the vast and wonderful fields of meditation, healing, mysticism, or spirituality. I believe we are simply translating the same transcendent experience into different metaphors.

These are a few of my favorite things…

The Foundations

Holy Bible, The: Revised Standard Version. Toronto, New York, Edinburgh: Thomas Nelson and Sons, 1952. It may just be because this is the version I grew up with, but I love the richness of the language.

Ballou, Robert O., et al., eds. *Bible of the World, The.* New York, Viking Press, 1948. This is the text book from "Comparing the World's Religions," a freshman course in which I found eye-widening readings that felt familiar and beloved, but foreign. It covers Hindu, Buddhist, Confucian, Taoist, Zoroastrian, Judeo-Christian, and Mohammedan scriptures. A simply wonderful book, to be sought in old book stores or a big library.

Rimpoche, Sogyal. *The Tibetan Book of Living and Dying.* Gaffney, Patrick and Andrew Harvey, eds. San Francisco, Harper, 1994. My two sisters and I undertook reading this book during the long months when our mother was dying. Mom suffered from Alzheimer's disease and recognized us but did not know who we were. We didn't know of any books from the Western religious traditions that discussed the dying process, so we turned to this book as coming from an ancient tradition that we honored, even if we weren't practitioners.

Books on the Alpha State

Conner, Janet. *Writing Down Your Soul; How to Activate and Listen to the Extraordinary Voice Within.* San Francisco. Conari Press, 2008. In this charmed and charming book, Janet Conner speaks to a Voice, gets responses, and teaches you how to do the same, with dramatic results. And with humor: "Dear Voice: I thought I wanted something, but no matter what I do, it isn't happening. Is this bad luck or good guidance? How can I tell?" [Note bene: this is not a book on journaling!]

Harvey, Richard. *The Flight of Consciousness: A Contemporary Map for the Spiritual Journey.* London: Ashgrove Publishing, 2002. This is a lovely guide to discovering who you are at the current point in your journey, and leading you to find ways to express who you can become.

Hofstadter, Douglas R. and Daniel C. Dennett. *The Mind's I.* New York: Bantam Books, 1981. A delightful collection of essays on existentialism.

McLaren, Karla. *Emotional Genius: Discovering the deepest language of the soul.* Columbia, CA: Laughing Tree Press, 2001. This is the most important book I have ever read: it taught me how to stop dissociating. An empath and healer, Karla carefully describes each emotion, telling the purpose the emotion serves in your life, and how to respect it and help it do its job. She gives detailed instructions on what to do to get rid of old emotions and how to handle new situations as they come up. With deep compassion, and the knowledge born of personal experience, Karla serves as a midwife as you acknowledge and release old hurts and get on with the joyful business of living a new life.

————Your Aura & Your Chakras: The Owner's Manual. Boston, MA: Weiser Books, 1998. This lovely little book describes your aura and chakras, and how to tell if they are in good working order. If you have been shutting down some aspects of yourself, your chakras may need your love and attention. Karla tells you how to give to yourself so that you can live a full life and give to others.

Silva, Jose. Mind Control, The Basic Lecture Series. Laredo, Texas, Silva Mind Control International, 1977. This workbook from the Mind Control lectures may not be available without taking the course. At least, that is how I got the book. And the course is wonderful. While the information is presented in a non-religious context, there is a deep spirituality behind these secular avenues into the Alpha state.

————*Reflections, Personal Evaluation by the Founder of the Silva Mind Control Method.* Laredo, Texas: The Institute of Psychorientology, 1981. Mr. Silva's personal statements, and interesting information about changes that participants experienced following their participation in Mind Control seminars.

Religious Meditation

Anderson , Sherry Ruth and Patricia Hopkins. *The Feminine Face of God: The Unfolding of the Sacred in Women.* New York: Bantam Books, 1991. A personal history of two women who sought a feminine way to worship. Through worship they find some answers for the problems of humankind. Beautifully written; a real inspiration.

Bancroft, Anne. *The Spiritual Journey,* Shaftsbury, Dorset, Rockport, Massachusetts: Element, 1991. Rich in content and easily read, this book leads you on a journey by comparing Eastern and Western religions in order to search for a new vision of spirituality.

Boucher, Sandy. *Discovering Kwan Yin, Buddhist Goddess of Compassion.* Boston: Beacon Press, 1999. This book includes both a history of the many forms Kwan Yin has taken in Buddhist cultures and suggestions for chants and meditations for those who want to include Kwan Yin in their daily practice.

De Carteret, Nikki. *Soul Power; the Transformation that happens when you know.* Alresford, Hants, U.K.: O Books, 2003. A lovely book about the changes that can occur from deep meditation.

Kelsey, Morton T. *The Other Side of Silence.* New York, Paramus, N.J., Toronto: Paulist Press, 1976. Kelsey provides a fascinating account of Christian meditation and cautions respect for its power. By leading you through accounts of the lives of mystical orders, Kelsey gives a model for some of the purposes of meditation.

Moore, Thomas. *Care of the Soul: A Guide for Cultivating Depth and Sacredness in Everyday Life.* New York: Harper Collins, 1992. In this exquisite and thought-provoking book, Moore suggests ways to find richness in life by using our inner promptings and ways to hear the calls from our souls.

———*The Re-Enchantment of Everyday Life.* New York: Harper Perennial,1986. Moore looks at those every-day things that can nourish our internal lives, and presents them to us so we may see them in a new light. A lovely book. Both richly scholarly and deeply nourishing.

New Age Physics

Zukav, Gary. *Dancing Wu Li Masters, The.* New York: William Morrow, 1979. Concepts of quantum physics can be graceful, when presented by this brilliant author. Of all the books I've read, this is the one I most wished I knew someone else who was also reading it at the same time. It is somewhat hard to read on your own, but worth it. I think this was the first book in which I found physics, laughter, and spirituality all in the same room, and on excellent speaking terms.

————*The Seat of the Soul.* New York: Simon & Schuster, 1989. Another deeply nourishing book that leaps from physics into the spiritual. This book is the most beautifully grounding reading.

————*Soul Stories.* New York, New York: Simon and Schuster, 2000. When my daughter-in-law died in her early 30's, she and my son had already been divorced. Her death left a chasm in the emotional life of my beloved grandchildren, who were young teens at the time. At one point while they were still in active grief, I read them a couple selections from this book because the stories are so touching and so full of hope. I then left the book in the living room where they sleep when they stay over with Gramma. Almost three years later my granddaughter was looking for something to read, and I pulled out this book. She said: "I remember that book! You read us part of it, and after you went to bed, I read all the rest of the stories out loud to my brother!"

Readings in Medicine and Psychology

Benson, Herbert, with Marg Stark. *Timeless Healing: The Power and Biology of Belief.* New York: A Fireside Book, Published by Simon & Shuster, 1997. The author of The Relaxation Response presents evidence from scientific studies that we have the power to heal ourselves. His studies also reveal that a large percentage of the American public believes in a higher power, and believes in the possibility of spiritual healing. I loved reading that! It helps me feel less lonely.

Borysenko, Joan. *Fire in the Soul: A New Psychology of Spiritual Optimism.* New York: Warner Books, 1993. Borysenko shows how we can integrate those things that have wounded us most deeply and change them into a life-view that is positive and uplifting. Transformative!

Chopra, Deepak. *Quantum Healing: Exploring the Frontiers of Mind/Body Medicine.* New York, New York: Bantam Books, 1990. Insight into how we can heal.

————*Unconditional Life: Discovering the Power to Fulfill Your Dreams.* New York: Bantam Books, 1992.

Dossey, Larry, M.D. *Recovering the Soul.* New York: Bantam Books, 1989. Dossey works on the premise that the mind does not exist within a body, but is "nonlocal," and is outside time and space. He explores evidence from medicine, religion, shamanism, and physics to provide a foundation for spirituality.

Liebman, Joshua Loth. *Peace of Mind.* New York: A Signet Book, New American Library, 1946. Liebman was a Rabbi and scholar who had a gift for providing entry-points into mysticism through normal experiences. In looking at psychology, he finds pathways to spirituality. A lovely little book.

Myss, Caroline. *Anatomy of the Spirit: The Seven Stages of Power and Healing.* New York: Three Rivers Press, 1996. If you have not read this, you have missed something very special. Caroline Myss combines her tale of personal and spiritual growth as a psychic healer with an in-depth analysis of Christianity, Judaism, and Buddhism. She finds parallel structures in the three religions, and synthesizes the core beliefs into a theory of how we can use our energy systems (chakras) to attain complete health and access to our spirituality. This is an amazing work that I have reread multiple times over several years.

————*Sacred Contracts: Awakening Your Divine Potential.* New York, New York: Three Rivers Press, 2002, 2003. This is a text on archetypes and a workbook that demonstrates how to define your personal archetypal patterns. It emphasizes how to use the energy that is provided by your chakras to focus your life on identifying and following your own path.

Orloff, Judith. *Second Sight: A Psychiatrist Clairvoyant Tells Her Extraordinary Story… and Shows You How to Discover Your Psychic*

Gifts. New York: Warner Books, 1996. A fascinating book by a psychic who has both an M.D. degree and a PhD in psychiatry. Her struggles to merge the information she receives psychically with her medical training speak to the ways in which a psychic must struggle in Western culture.

Pert, Candace B. *Molecules of Emotion: Why You Feel the Way You Feel.* New York: Scribner, 1997. This captivating book recounts Dr. Pert's struggle to learn as well as her political struggle to get credit for her work in a male-dominated subculture of enormous power. My Western-science based, skeptical mind feels grounded when encountering the molecular reasons for something previously dismissed as "merely emotional." A book full of "Ah-ha!"

Reincarnation and Life After Life

Berman, Phillip L. *The Journey Home: What Near-Death Experiences and Mysticism Teach Us About the Gift of Life.* New York: Pocket Books 1996. Moving stories of people who have been near death but been revived.

Cannon, Dolores. *Between Death and Life.* Huntsville, Arizona. Ozark Mountain Publishing, 1993. Fascinating details about the life between lives given by people who Dolores Cannon has hypnotized. These are direct transcripts of both the hypnotized subject and Ms. Cannon's questions and comments about them. For the most part, the descriptions they give are amazingly similar to what Emmanuel Swedenborg describes in his book Heaven and Hell; see "Emmanuel Swedenborg and His Works" later in this chapter.

Goldberg, Bruce. *Past Lives, Future Lives.* New York: Ballantine Books, 1982. Dr. Goldberg uses hypnotherapy to regress his patients to previous lives in the hopes of finding the cause for unremitting medical symptoms in this life. He takes the explorations of other lives into the future. Interesting, whether you follow him there or not.

Monroe, Robert A. *Ultimate Journey*. New York: Doubleday, 1994. This book, about out-of-body experiences, provides a map and directions for this kind of travel. It seeks to provide answers to questions you may have about "where you were" when you were meditating or dreaming. Elizabeth Kubla-Ross' endorsement of this book helped me trust it as a possible guide. But in all such matters, it is an individual decision whether to travel a path, and if so, how far you want to go.

Moody, Jr., Raymond. *Life After Life*. New York: Bantam Books, 1977. Dr. Moody describes experiences of people who had been declared clinically dead but then been revived. These people recounted vivid trips into the afterlife. Their journeys are consistent with others who have experienced the same thing. These memories include passing through a tunnel, meeting loved ones who have died previously, and meeting a Being of Light. In one interesting chapter he finds parallels in *The Bible,* Plato, *The Tibetan Book of the Dead,* and Emmanuel Swedenborg's writings. This little book is a keystone to my personal beliefs, and was deeply meaningful to me at several times when my beliefs were tested.

Newton, Michael. *Journey of Souls, Case Studies of Life Between Lives*. St. Paul, Minnesota: Llewellyn Publications, 1996. Dr. Newton uses past-age regression with his therapy clients; this book provides case studies of the journeys reported by these clients when they were "regressed to the time before you last incarnated." After studying many sessions, Dr. Newton discovered similarities in what was reported to him, and presents these along with the transcribed sessions with the clients. Fascinating reading.

————*Destiny of Souls, New Case Studies of Life Between Lives*. St. Paul, Minnesota: Llewellyn Publications, 2000. Additional information about how we exist in spirit and evaluate our past and future lives. Interesting examination of how we can learn from other souls who have hurt us in this life, and how they learn from the same experiences. There is a huge amount of rich detail about the processes and the reasons for the struggles we experience during our lives on the planet: we are challenged so that we can learn.

Ring, Kenneth. *Heading Toward Omega: In Search of the Meaning of the Near-Death Experience.* New York: Quill, William Morrow, 1984. Dr. Ring has studied both the near-death experience itself and what happens after that experience to the people who have gone through it. This very readable, personal account is full of the moving stories told by those who have had a near-death experience.

Symbols and Dreams

Jung, Carl. *Man and His Symbols.* New York: Doubleday and Co., 1964. Jung's view that all mankind shares symbols at a deep level is very grounding. It adds a great richness of insight into any search for meaning.

Shelly, Violet. *Symbols and the Self.* Virginia Beach, Virginia: A.R.E. Press, 1976. Starting with symbols as simple as a straight line and a circle, this book suggests meanings that we can find in our dreams and in the visions that occur while we are in meditation. While each of us has unique meanings associated with symbols, there is a commonality that is provided by the culture in which we have lived our lives. This is a tiny, very accessible book to keep with your dream journal.

On the Subject of Healing

Campion, Lisa. *The Art of Psychic Reiki: Developing your Intuitive Abilities for Energy Healing*. Oakland, CA: Reveal Press, An Imprint of New Harbinger Publications, Inc. 2018. This delightful book leads you through ways to harness your psychic abilities when you are meditating and practicing Reiki for healing. It could have saved me many an hour of concern had it been published years ago when I was meditating for healing with Tom. Conversely, Ms. Campion's thesis that the very act of practicing healing opens up psychic activity in your life is certainly borne out by my experience.

Cerminara, Gina. *Many Lives, Many Loves*. New York: A Signet Book, New American Library, 1963. A lovely small book on reincarnation and how knowing about your past lives can help explain and extricate you from issues in your current experience. Easily read and thought-provoking.

Hammond, Sally. *We Are All Healers*, New York: Ballantine Books, 1973. Ms. Hammond has experienced the power of spiritual healing and introduces the reader to some of the leaders in the field. This book is about her voyage into spiritual healing.

Kubler-Ross, Elizabeth. *On Death and Dying*, Collier Books, 1997. Dr. Kubler-Ross works with terminally ill patients; her work and the Hospice movement have helped bring healing (despite the absence of a physical cure) into the lives of the dying.

———*The Tunnel and The Light: Essential Insights on Living and Dying*. Dr. Kubler-Ross uses material from her own life as well as experiences with dying patients to describe the way symbols and mystical experiences give depth to the meaning of life.

———and David Kessler. *Life Lessons: Two Experts on Death and Dying Teach Us About the Mysteries of Life and Living*. New York: Scribner, 2000. This wonderful collaboration describes how all of life's aspects (love, authenticity, power, guilt, and forgiveness) help us accomplish the work we have come to the planet to do. When we do this work, we heal a deep place in our souls. This amazing little book tells us how.

Puryear, Meredith Ann. *Healing through Meditation and Prayer.* Virginia Beach, Virginia: A.R.E. Press, 1978. This small book covers meditation, affirmations, prayer, attitudes, the laying on of hands, and laws of spiritual healing.

Sanford, Agnes. *The Healing Light: The Art and Method of Spiritual Healing.* St. Paul, Minnesota: Macalester Park Publishing Co., 1947. Ms. Sanford is a devout Christian who uses her faith to lead others into healing. A little instruction book that tells of lovely healings, and provides you with the steps to follow.

Worrall, Ambrose A. and Olga N. Worrall. *The Gift of Healing.* New York: Harper and Row, Publishers, 1976. When the medical profession has abandoned some patients, they have sought help from the Worralls, and the Worralls have been able to help. Mr. and Mrs. Worrall live a life of religious commitment to provide these gifts to those in need, and to speak and write in order to teach others how to perform spiritual healing.

Emmanuel Swedenborg and His Works

Emmanuel Swedenborg (1688-1772) was a scholar and civil engineer for the first fifty years of his life. Then he had a transformative experience that led him to the belief that he should translate the Bible because it was not being correctly understood. So, he tackled this arduous task, translating line-by-line through many thousands of lines of text. He felt he was guided, receiving direct input into what the text should read.

Later he felt that his assignment changed, and he started writing about the many mystical experiences that he had, including visits to both Heaven

118

and Hell. The content of his visions was not only startlingly different from the dogma of the Lutheran Church, of which he was a member, but highly critical of Lutheran church practices.

He stated that there is a place in Heaven for people of all faiths, a heretical statement in a day when Lutherans denounced both Catholics and Jews. He described in detail how we are not judged in Heaven, because God is all-loving, but rather we continue on in the afterlife to the place where our paths had been leading during our time on earth. Thus, sinners of all stripes prefer the company of other sinners and their sinful activities, and choose to take themselves to the place called Hell. But those who have been trying to live lives of usefulness and love continue into Heaven.

As I read deeper, I found so many specifics that helped me understand my visions. We continue in a recognizable form in the afterlife, and can communicate with those who were left behind. We communicate in direct thought transfer, not needing spoken words, but also not being able to hide our feelings. The ultimate source of all love is waiting for us in Heaven.

In addition to the books Swedenborg wrote, there are many books written about Swedenborg's philosophy, some of which are also included below.

Kirven, Robert H. *Angels in Action; What Swedenborg Saw and Heard.* West Chester, Pennsylvania: Chrysalis Books; Imprint of the Swedenborg Foundation, 1995. This lovely book describes how angels surround us our whole lives, prompting us toward lives of service and helping to protect us from evil. Kirven tells how we, as deeply spiritual beings, must use our free will with a pure heart.

Swedenborg, Emmanuel. *Heaven and its Wonders and Hell; Drawn from Things Heard and Seen.* Translated from the Latin by George F Dole. West Chester, Pennsylvania: Swedenborg Foundation, 2000. Although it is a very large book (454 pages of text in this translation) it is the book many people read first to get acquainted with Swedenborg's writings. Swedenborg provides countless details of what life is like in Heaven, such as how time as we know it does not exist, how we instantly understand each other's thoughts, how an angel is made up of equal parts of a man and a woman, and how the Sun in heaven represents God's presence. Swedenborg wrote all his books in Latin; this book is an especially graceful translation.

————*Divine Love and Wisdom.* Translated by George F. Dole. West Chester, Pennsylvania: Swedenborg Foundation, 1985. Swedenborg posited that God is the source of all love and wisdom, and that we only exist by virtue of that love. Because God loves us, he wants us to love him in return. Thus, he provides us with free will because we can only love another from a free state—it is meaningless if the love is forced. In attempting to live good lives, we must find ways to be useful citizens and family members, and allow God's love to come through our loving acts to one another.

Swedenborg, Emanuel, and James F. Lawrence. *Awaken from Death: an inspiring description of the soul's journey into the spiritual realms upon bodily death.* Newtonville, MA. 2005. J. Appleseed & Co. This book is divided into two parts: The first section is excerpted from Swedenborg's Heaven and Hell. This section provides the amazing detail with which Swedenborg relates how a person lives a life that will lead to Heaven, what happens in Heaven, and how selfish and evil people condemn themselves to Hell. It includes some of the most tender descriptions of how lovingly angels help new arrivals in the spirit world. The second portion of the book, called "Swedenborg's Epic Journey" describes Swedenborg's remarkable civil and scientific achievements and his writing prior to his spiritual transformation. It also relates Swedenborg's famous clairvoyant visions and the result of these experiences on his life in society. The book closes with a moving tribute from Helen Keller.

Woofenden, Lee, *Death and Rebirth: From near death experiences to eternal life.* Middleboro, MA: New Christian Era Ministries, 2009. This charming book carefully compares the events listed in Near Death experiences with the way that Emanuel Swedenborg describes the dying experience. Using references from Raymond Moody's Life After Life, Kenneth Ring's Life at Death, and others, Woofenden finds striking parallels throughout Swedenborg's writings. He describes the initial phases when we first leave our body, the passage through darkness, meeting family and friends who have previously died, and seeing angels and a vision of light. It is simply a stunning little book.

————*On Earth As It Is In Heaven: Reflections on Jesus' Parables of the Kingdom and Emanuel Swedenborg's Heaven and Hell.* Middleboro, MA: New Christian Era Ministries, 2005. This book is composed of a series of sermons that reflect on the Lord's Prayer and how we can live a life on earth as if we were in Heaven.

Edgar Cayce's A.R.E.

The Association of Research and Enlightment (A.R.E.) was founded by Edgar Cayce, an American twentieth century mystic whose Christian faith was stretched by his trance-state learnings about meditation, healing, the Akashic records, and reincarnation. The A.R.E. has its own publishing house; see www://http.are-cayce.com where you can learn of the association's activities. I first learned to meditate in an A.R.E. "Search for God" group that met weekly to read the Bible and hold a healing meditation. I refer to that group many times in this book.

Puryear, Herbert B. *Reflections on the Path.* Virginia Beach, Virginia: A.R.E. Press, 1979. Like many other books from the A.R.E. Press, this book seeks to translate Edgar Cayce's readings into practices that we can follow in our daily lives. There is a lot of depth here for people who want to walk that particular path.

Sechrist, Elsie. *Meditation: Gateway to Light.* Virginia Beach, Virginia: A.R.E. Press, 1972. This Christian book quotes the Bible and the Cayce trance recordings about equally. It presents an approach to meditation that includes the body's energy centers (chakras). Leafing through this book 20-some years later, it reads like a primer. It gave me a lovely place to start my search, and I am very grateful.

————*Dreams, Your Magic Mirror*. New York: Warner Books, 1974. This book combines techniques to use to remember and interpret your dreams, as well as interpretations of dreams that were submitted to Edgar Cayce.

Study Group of the A. R. E., compilers. *A Search for God, Parts I and II.* Virginia Beach, Virginia: A.R.E. Press, 1970. These books were created by the original Edgar Cayce Study Group, and have been used by generations of Study Groups to follow the path.

Thurston, Mark A. *Experiments in a Search for God.* Virginia Beach, Virginia: A.R.E. Press, 1976. This book is used in the Edgar Cayce study groups as a supplement to A Search for God.

————*How to Interpret Your Dreams: Practical Techniques Based on the Edgar Cayce Readings.* Virginia Beach, Virginia: ARE Press, 1978. An insightful book that covers many aspects of dreaming, from dreams that reflect bodily desires to meeting the Divine in dreams.

6 Endnotes

Chapter One

1.   Otis Reading, "Respect," Atlantic Records, Muscle Shoals Sound Studios, © 1969.

2.   Quarterflash, The Album, "Harden my Heart." The David Geffen Company, © 1981.

Chapter Three

1.   Rev. Sarah Buteux, "Giving from the Heart" www.swedenborgchapel.org Readings: Sermons and Addresses.

7 Afterward

Thanks for joining me for these tales of how my life has spun its threads and woven its cloth of joy and mystery. Here are some final thoughts, and my email address so you can get in touch, and let me know what amazing things happen in your life!

Who Am I?

I'm Rosey, and I wrote this book about forty-five mystical events that really happened, much to my surprise. I recorded them at the time so I would remember them exactly. I didn't want my faulty memory to change anything that happened, but I also didn't want to forget any details, or diminish how shocking these things were when they happened.

Over the years I meditated frequently, and sometimes I got answers in my meditations to the questions that these events raised. Some answers came in my dreams. Many answers came from the hundreds of books I read about spirituality and its associated topics.

My day job was a very satisfactory career as a technical writer for the computer industry. I did not like working for large companies, but the drawback with startups is that sometimes they didn't actually get started. Instead, they folded, and I would be looking for a new job again! During my tech writing career, I was responsible for literally thousands of pages of user documentation. It was hard work, but I loved it! And once, when I entered one of my books in a contest held by the Society of Technical Communicators, I won a prestigious award. I was pretty proud of that book, and thrilled that the judges felt the same way!

Just for the record, I know that these "About the Author" blurbs are usually written about the author as a third party ("While Lawson was associated with…"). But I spent my three decades in tech writing fighting the "passive voice" syndrome (where you would write: "the key should be pressed," instead of "Press the key."). So I don't want to give up that fight now. Especially in a piece about me! Hope you like that change.

I would love to hear from you! What stories particularly spoke to you? Have you had any similar experiences? You can reach me at newwingspublishers@gmail.com .

What Am I to do with this Knowledge?

Tom came back to console me after he died. Among other things, he told me that time in Heaven was spent learning and working on projects. But as days, then months, and then years go by after Tom's visit, I discover that I have to mature into the knowledge that he gave me. I don't begin to understand its implications at the time. I do know that I have suddenly received an immense truth about life: that the afterlife is a vibrant state that I will love. That is huge!

The first result of that knowledge is that I become totally unafraid of death. The second, also huge result, is that I can look forward to being with Tom forever! I have not lost him forever, we will be together forever! It makes the current separation many degrees more bearable.

But there are implications in what Tom said that are even greater. When Tom described how their time was spent, I had never heard of anything resembling that description of Heaven. I wasn't sure that I even believed in Heaven. But Tom told me of a place where I could look forward to continue doing things that I loved doing here on Earth. How amazing! And how wonderful!

Many years after Tom died, I came upon the writings of Emanuel Swedenborg. I was awestruck as I read about a Heaven incredibly similar to what Tom described! (See "Ex Libris" for descriptions of Swedenborg's works.)

There is another aspect to what Tom said, as well. He left me with what I have come to realize is a rock-solid belief system that is based on fact. I don't just *believe* in the afterlife; I *know* that it exists.

I have always doubted people who claimed to know about such things, and now I find myself in that category which I have disavowed all my life. I cannot simultaneously hold those beliefs to be true and remain a skeptic! So, I guess I have to resign from my prideful skeptical state. It is with amazement that I do so, and with another parallel new belief. I do not expect you to believe these things merely because I do. But I also no longer feel I should hide my own beliefs, just because you might hold different ones or maintain a skeptical stance of your own.

So, with my matured understanding of what Tom's messages imply, it is time to share them. I hope you find comfort, as I did, in his words.

Why Am I Publishing this Book Now?

I had the experiences in this book when I was in my late twenties and early thirties. I am now in my eighties! Why do I want to publish this book now?

At the time I was experiencing the things in this book, I was working at a job that demanded lots of extra hours in the week. I was also a mother of two teenage sons. While Tom was still with us, he and I spent a lot of time meditating together for his health and working on his photography business.

After Tom died, I was still self-supporting. I transitioned from being a master teacher to being a technical writer, and eventually head of the documentation department for a number of small computer companies. There was not a huge amount of time to devote to this book after I'd spent my whole day writing and getting those technical manuals through the publication process.

But throughout those many years I exclusively read books on spirituality, synchronicity, meditation, and dreams. And as I did, I would come upon something that I had experienced and written about in my Journal.

For instance, I remember the thrill I felt when I read somebody else describe souls as being surrounded by beautiful glistening bubbles. That's how I saw the souls in the story "A Blessing for the Teacher." And I was startled when I read about somebody having an out of body experience. But that was nothing compared to how I felt during my own out of body experience, in "A Near Miss on a Drive to the Airport."

Up until the time I would find these links to others' experiences, I felt a disconnect: I knew what I had experienced, for absolute certainty. And I had been very conscientious in trying to describe exactly what it was like, with no exaggeration or hyperbole. But the nagging question "How could that be true?" was with me all the time. It was one of the reasons I recorded the events, so I could capture all the details and then try to find meaning and understanding in the whole story.

Once I had a sense of validation by finding a similar experience in another author's writings, I felt less lonely. I felt vindicated by no longer being "the only one" who had experienced something so far out of the realm of normalcy!

So, to wrap up the question I posed earlier in this chapter, now that I'm retired, and I have experienced validation from other authors, I feel that I want to share these events and their meanings. I want you who come after me to be able to find validation for your own experiences in these pages.

May many blessings come to you as you search for the deeper meanings in your life.